G000124419

Game, Guns, and American Infatuation

Game, Guns, and American Infatuation

Anita Cortez

Owl Canyon Press

© 2022 by Anita Cortez
Cover painting by Frank Cortez

First Edition, 2022
All Rights Reserved
Library of Congress Cataloging-in-Publication Data

Cortez, Anita
Game, Guns, and American Infatuation—1st ed.
p. cm.

ISBN: 978-1-952085-19-2
Library of Congress Control Number: 2021951260

Owl Canyon Press
Boulder, Colorado

No part of this book may be reproduced in any form or by any electronic or mechanical means including information storage retrieval systems without permission in writing from the publisher, except by a reviewer, who may quote brief passages for review. Neither the authors, the publishers, nor its dealers or distributors shall be liable to the purchaser or any other person or entity with respect to any liability, loss, or damage caused or alleged to be caused directly or indirectly by this book.

For Jason
as he hunts for the *terroir* of his own roots
and for my father

Turning and turning in the widening gyre
the falcon cannot hear the falconer;
Things fall apart; the centre cannot hold…

W.B. Yeats

Table of Contents

PREFACE

People hunt for a lot of different reasons: some for the pure sport of the stalk and catch, some for survival, some out of boredom. Sometimes we find ourselves mandated to do it, either by governments or genetics. Sometimes we are horrified to find how much pleasure we derive from it. I knew a man once who told me how lost he was since coming home from Viet Nam. There was no rush like government-sanctioned killing, he said. He muddled through his life here in the heartland until he couldn't any longer and put a bullet through his head rather than someone else's. The final rush.

The first time I met the man with whom I would eventually spend the second half of my life, I had no idea our meeting would lead me to this book. I was a non-traditional student—one of those women who come back to school once their own children are in school. I was after more than a degree. I was eager to learn, to explore, to find out what I thought, what I wanted out of life. In short, I had come back to find out who I was and who I could become.

I signed up for a poetry course because I had always enjoyed writing and reading. I had had limited opportunities for furthering my education as I had followed my first husband around the globe in the military. After the military years, I remained limited to family by finances and responsibilities. It was not until my son was in elementary school and my husband in veterinary school that I found time and financial aid to go to school myself.

By this time I had seen some of the world, and I was tired of the banality of homemaking. So I signed up for poetry. I remember telling this poetry professor that I wanted to write about rainbows and butterflies. I wanted to think about *pretty* things. *Prettiness.*

"Where did you grow up?" he responded, ignoring my heartfelt divulgence.

"Wyoming," I replied.

"That's frightening," he remarked. "They carry guns there, don't they?"

"Where did *you* grow up?" I asked, somewhat defensively.

"New Jersey," he responded.

I wondered what kind of a jerk this guy was that he would think Wyoming more frightening than New Jersey.

Many years later after we had bridged our differences or discovered our similarities and embarked upon a life together, he wrote a memoir which he entitled *Guns and Boyhood in America*. I always thought that odd because, in fact, his boyhood had been pretty far removed from guns, toy or otherwise. He came from a highly intellectual family and learned early on to consider the aesthetics of the world around him. His book is about art and considering. It is not a book about guns.

The more we considered our lives and our aesthetics, the more I came to realize that *I* was the one who had something to say about guns. Although, or perhaps because I was female, and although I grew up the youngest of three girls, in a white, shingled house, daughter of a railroader and a teacher, an aesthetic of "western individualism" had informed my perspective more than I had known.

I did not grow up on a ranch. I did not grow up riding horses. I had no brothers. The only man in our house was my father. My only male companion was the boy next door. How, then, did guns creep into my lexicon? And what did they represent for me as a child growing up, and later, as an adult looking back, how did they inform my life?

I took that poetry class, and eventually I coaxed a poem about a rainbow out of myself. To my amazement, however, the rainbow was a trout! Not at all what I had expected. Slowly but inevitably, I began to realize that I had to write what was inside of me, for better or for worse.

My father was also a big influence on me. He babysat me while my mother taught school since he worked the evening shift as a telegrapher for the Burlington Northern Railroad. It was only in later years, as a result of working with lots of people at a university, that I came to realize what an idyllic childhood I was afforded. Few people have had the childhood that I lived. I was given the gift of parents who loved each other and their daughters. And I was given the added privilege of being youngest daughter. That meant there was more money as I was growing up, therefore, fewer struggles and more leisure.

From early childhood, I had room to roam. I roamed the property from pasture fence to front gate, and I roamed my imagination from here to there. I was not hemmed in. I am certain, had I been born in another era, I would have been another sharp-shooting Annie Oakley, loving to compete with the man-boys, and loving the theatrics of it all. I was as comfortable in the skin of girl-child as I was in Daddy's boy. Smart kids, educators like to say, have options.

Now later in life, I like to think I have gained some perspective over what I am writing in these essays. I started out thinking I was writing about the past. Guns are not a part of my life these days. I live with a poet now instead of a hunter. I live in Kansas, not in Wyoming, and the times we currently live in certainly call into question the American infatuation with guns. I am not necessarily opposed to people owning guns. I have lived around too many hunters who hunted to feed their families. I was grateful myself for the freezer full of elk meat in the early years of marriage. I am myself not without the stain of the hunt.

These days I am more into browsing through bookstores or art galleries, hunting for the *Duenda* in musical experiences, and learning about the decadent pleasures of multi-starred restaurants. Hunting has been transformed for me.

I find that last statement curious: *Hunting has been transformed for me.* It is odd, don't you think, that it is the hunting that has undergone transformation and not the hunter? This is what I love and hate about writing. The discovery. The coming to terms, face-to-face, with oneself. The realization that hunting is so inbred in us that we are continually involved in the hunt whether we know it or not. Sometimes we are the hunter, sometimes the hunted. Prey and predator all at the same time.

Sometimes it is difficult to distinguish one from the other. Which "truth" is ours at any given moment? The poet William Wordsworth believed the writer needed the element of *time* in order to arrive at the truth of a matter. Time provided *distance* which, in turn, provided perspective, he thought. I would alter that notion slightly. I would say that time and distance provide *a* perspective, not *the* perspective, not the *ultimate* perspective. Perhaps a more complex perspective, much like aged wine, but still only *one* momentary perspective. Perspective, it seems, is constantly changing. *Spots in time*, Wordsworth would say.

What is the *truth* of these pages to follow? I can only promise you that these essays represent my story as I best know it and remember it, my past history, or as a feminist ideologist might say, *her-story*. Undoubtedly, I would have written these essays differently at the age of twenty or even thirty. I did not begin to examine my life until the age of forty when, like many women of my generation, I finally found a space of time for reflection. Undoubtedly, were my ex-spouse, or any other characters herein, to have written the stories, they would have a different slant. That's what history—*her*-story—is: a matter of perspective. And some viewpoints have been too long silenced. So who is to say which version, or whose version, is *the Truth*?

Might it be like the story of the blind men and the elephant? Might we all be hunting the same elephant but come upon it from different angles? Does my Truth negate another's Truth?

I write these episodes as my gift to my son, a chef, that he might know me better for the flawed stalker I am. I write them so that one day, when he is pondering his own hunt, how he got where he is, why the *terroir* of his cuisine is so important to him, he may understand a little better. His genes dictate to him. His grandfather is an artist. His father is a hunter and competitor. His mother? Perhaps he can flush her out of the pages that follow. He is himself a jazz trombonist turned chef of haute cuisine. He was born with the scent in his nostrils.

It doesn't seem to matter whether we are hunting for antelope or the perfect career path or the perfect aesthetic experience. We can search out peace or equity. We can hunt for mutual understanding. We can call it whatever we like, but we are all bound by the rules of the game: We must wander this earth as the animals we are. *Are you game?*

GAME

I grew up in northern Wyoming in the basin at the foot of the Bighorns. The badlands stretched to the horizon north and west of town and ambled in dry rivulets to the south as though taunting the fields of hay, alfalfa, sugar beets. The badlands are just that--no water to turn them green. Just patches of alkali white as snow in July, sage, anthills like miniature pyramids. And antelope. Antelope are the camels of the badlands. They thrive on scarcity. They give children and adults alike hope on a long drive through the badlands. "There's one! I saw one! Look! There's a mother and baby!" They are the proof that life does persist.

Come early fall, however, the antelope suddenly disappear. You can drive for hours and never see a single one. You could almost convince yourself, were you actually looking specifically for them, that they were purely mythical animals of the underworld. Persephone's playmates.

But if you are a hunter, as most men and many women in Wyoming seem to be, you are not so easily given to such fantasy. You are a realist. The antelope have not run off to the Netherland. They are game and it is hunting season. All it takes is a gunshot or two resonating through the ravines to make game head for the most distant horizon.

If you are hunting for antelope, it is wise to be out early on the first day. That is your one good chance. If you are a seasoned hunter, you have been driving the back roads, wandering the hills and ravines for weeks in advance trying to figure out the routine of the game. Where are they abundant, where scarce? Are there does, bucks? What are their established pathways? Where do they go for water?

And then you study the land. Where do the gullies lead? What's over each hill? You wish you had taken word problems more seriously: If Mark and Les approach from the north, from Marker 18, in the pickup, going approximately fifteen miles an hour at five-thirty in the morning, and George and Leo approach on foot from two hills away, leaving at four a.m., they will arrive simultaneously at the far ravine at approximately what angle of the sun? Then you must ask, from what direction does the breeze blow? Their scent will be carried downwind in which direction? How far will sound carry at thirty degrees?

Any self-respecting Wyoming hunter knows to go for the head. One clean shot straight to the brain before the game knows what has happened. The trick is to get to the brain before fear has a chance to register. Fear telegraphs adrenaline throughout the body so that later, when you eat the meat, no matter how you try to dress it up, you get the taste of fear in every bite.

This is the game that city hunters know. These are sportsmen from out of state. Some of them will pay outrageous prices for the opportunity to kill. The kill is what matters to them. Most of the meat will spoil on the way home because the animal hasn't been gutted on site and straddles the front grill of a sports utility vehicle like so much squashed bug. They probably won't eat the meat anyway unless it is to serve one-time-only *hors d'oeuvres* at a massive gourmet tasting party. They will serve plenty of good dry red wine or bourbon and stories of near peril to wash it down. They will send the head off to a recommended taxidermist who is well known for bringing the head to life. The head will be hung in the den amidst leather, mahogany, and many a sweet deal.

Then there are the locals. Locals are not sportsmen. They are hunters. They hunt to fill their freezers for the winter. They hunt antelope, deer, elk. They hunt to reconfirm their place in the family: father, son, grandson. Ontogeny recapitulating phylogeny. The whole family prepares. The women finish the canning from the garden. They pack quarts of mixed vegetables for stews; they can tomatoes. They pack dried fruits and nuts in baggies to stuff into pockets of hunting shirts. They bake homemade breads, some stuffed with meat fillings and fruit fillings, some multi-grain for toast and sandwiches. They bake individual pies using the remaining mincemeat from last year's hunt and each man and boy will find his favorite cookies to remind him of the good wife, mom, grandma who will be at home with a warm bath and a home-cooked meal just waiting for his return from the hunt.

There will be no cocktail parties with fine red wine and cognac when they come home. Their socializing happens at the camp. They swap stories--how the old man's son learned the lesson about where not to shoot a deer, how the old man made him climb down the canyon and carry the deer out on his back; how the old man once shot a bull elk by mistake when he had a license for a cow, but the bull was dead, wasn't no way that bull was coming back from the dead, and sometimes it's only ethical to turn a bull into a cow with a little cosmetic surgery; and the young boy contents himself with the stories of his elders and soaks up the smells of firewood and rawhide and fresh baked bread. His stories will develop over the dinner table this coming winter. He may become known as "Little Doc, the surgeon's assistant," which will always be accompanied with a wink.

I grew up around guns. Although I came from a family of all girls, my father was a hunter. He had rifles and shotguns. He had a handgun or two I remember seeing once or twice in his possession, but I didn't like them. Whenever he brought them out, my mother got nervous and her voice was hushed and she wore a look of disapproval on her face. My father would wear the look of a defiantly naughty boy as he held the gun in his hand, and it wouldn't be long until the gun was quietly gone from sight. Long guns, on the other hand, were just there. I knew they were hidden in my parents' closet. I knew that I was never allowed to touch them. And I knew that that rule was unequivocal. I touched many things in my parents' closet. I knew that my eldest sister hid her mannequin doll and her favorite baby doll from me there. And a few years later, I knew that my mother hid her teacher's edition of my math book under the pile of bed linens. I sampled all the bottles of Avon I found there. I tried on both my mother and my father's shoes. My fingerprints were all over that small closet, but not one fingerprint ever landed on my father's guns.

I can't say that I was afraid of the guns. I just had a healthy respect instilled in me. Guns were like a well-seasoned, walnut-bowled pipe and Prince Albert tobacco. They were hands off. They were man things. I wasn't interested. I was the youngest in a family of girls. I played dolls and house, I made mud pies and decorated them with crayon shavings, I danced on the great expanse of lawn, lilac sprigs in my hair, swaying with the breeze to my cottonwood partners. I was girl-child personified, a personification of a personification. I lived in my imagination much of the time, as I was between six and nine years younger than my sisters who had lives with their older friends.

I was also final child, my parents nearing middle-age at my birth. Perhaps it was the fact that I was so much younger than my sisters; perhaps it was my father's knowing that he would never have a male child; perhaps it was merely what all children, left to their own imaginings will come to, but I wandered quite easily from female world into male domain and back again. One summer I carved Yellowstone Park into the side of the hill behind the garage. Using baking soda and food coloring from the kitchen, I fashioned mud pots and even got Old Faithful to make some gallant sputterings. I carved Yellowstone Canyon and painted it orange, yellow and red, but the waterfall kept washing the color down in rivulets that turned into ravines. Morning Glory Pool was a bright turquoise blue and Sylvan Lake was a deep, impenetrable green. I even started a forest fire by burning some dried weed trees with a magnifying glass and then quickly extinguishing it with water from the lake. Throughout the park, my plastic brown bears roamed, backing up toy cars for miles on end. Farm cows became buffalo, horses turned into moose, little girl to boy.

Cap guns were a favorite of mine also. I loved the noise I could make with them as I crawled through the tall pasture grasses in ambush of anything *other*. And most of all, I loved taking an entire reel of caps and pounding it hard, stone on stone, to get the loudest pop I could muster. I loved the smell of gunpowder and sometimes I could even elicit a spark.

Gunpowder quickened my blood. It did not frighten me. Even when at dinner around the oval dining table, as our family sat, father, mother, and three little girls, eating meatloaf and orange-carrot jello salad and saying things like, "May I please have some more kool-aid?" or "Frances kicked me under the table!"--even when my father would suddenly jump up from the table and disappear into the bedroom to return with a shotgun in hand, I was not afraid. I would watch him stealthily tiptoe around the dining table, fish a shotgun shell out of his pocket and plunk it in place. I would watch as he paced and stalked and timed his attack through the window. Sometimes he would ease open the door just a crack, motioning absolute silence from us, then wait, frozen just long enough to be forgotten. Sometimes he would go to the door, hesitate, then suddenly throw it open and blast away, setting his sights on some pugnacious magpie who dared to taunt him outside the window. Rarely, if ever, did my father actually hit the bird. Instead it would fly just out of range and perch on the roof of an outbuilding as if to ridicule my father's poor aim. I would sit there at the table, my eyes glued to the gun, my hands covering my ears, my nostrils ready to receive the spice of gunpowder wafting over the family supper.

The guns rested in the gun rack of my dad's pickup truck when he would take Duffy, his Brittany spaniel, and me out for a run. Duffy, who was terrified of firecrackers, would come running and leap into the back of the truck at the sight of a gun. I would sit up on the seat of my dad's dusty old truck, bouncing along as the ruts dictated. We would wander off toward Beaver Creek or sometimes toward Timbercreek where a farmer had given his permission for my dad to hunt. We hunted pheasant or sometimes chukkers. My father would stop the truck alongside a dirt road and we would pile out, tramp across the reedy growth lining the road, jump irrigation ditches, and crawl cautiously through barbed wire fences to get into the field.

Once in the field Duffy would run far out ahead with me trailing behind him waving my arms in the air, my father's earthbound decoy. On a good morning Duffy and I might scare up two or three pheasants. They would rise out of the marshes into the air, a soft golden-brown flutter of life at the edge, and Duffy would stop dead on his heels, holding the point, this very moment, the moment he was bred for. My father might hit one or two birds. He would raise his shotgun to his shoulder, bring the scope to his brow, and pull the slide of shotgun back until the hard metallic clack dropped the shell into position, his body swiveling in unison with the shotgun as it tracked the fowl in flight. The air would explode against my ear, the pheasant might continue to fly for a partial breath, then seem to pause briefly in flight before falling silently into the reeds and dried grasses below. Duffy would spring into action, determined to track down the scent whether it led through field or pond. He would come trotting back, head held high, and delicately lay the limp bird at my father's feet. My father would praise his work and pat the spaniel heartily as he tucked the bird into the canvas game bag on his hip. I was superfluous then. The moment belonged to man and dog. I disappeared. Dissipated, I became pure scent: gunpowder stinging in nostril, rot of leaf and cow dung, murk of marsh, wet hair of dog, an over-scent of feathers no longer able to contain the wildness within.

Most men have mid-life crises where they act out against the rules society has imposed too early upon them. My father changed too. He put away the guns, and it wasn't until years later as a young wife that I became involved with guns again. Stan, my husband, was the son of a forest ranger. He had been raised to hunt. He had graduated from cap gun to Daisy Red Ryder to single shot twenty-two by early adolescence. Shotguns and rifles weren't far behind.

Every October was ritual. He and his father would get out the rifles, Remington .30-06 and Winchester .257, and oil them down, rubbing and polishing each to a smooth shine, swabbing out the bore with soft oiled rags. Minuscule screw drivers would litter the dining table as the men mounted and adjusted high-powered, wide-angled scopes and checked their accuracy for distance against some neighbor's cow, dog, or pickup in the farthest pasture. This is when the stories would start. Every year they were the same. Stan's name would change to Peach Pot, and then the entire story of how he ate the whole two-gallon can of peaches and all its consequences would spill out.

Talk would change to the game warden, and how he would arrest his own grandmother if he caught her hunting without a license. Laughter would turn to scorn. Where was the professional courtesy? Then the planning would begin. How many elk licenses did they have when all was said and done? How many cows, how many bulls? How many could they harvest at any one time? Where on the mountain had the game warden been spotted on a particular day? Did they need to take the women up to the cabin or could they afford to leave them behind? The first game of the hunt was for game warden.

I enjoyed the time in town where my parents now lived while the men traipsed all over the mountain. It was usually Halloween and my folks and I would take Jason trick-or-treating in their small town where everyone knew everyone else. It was one of the last bastions of the good haul where parents didn't have to worry what "treats" might be slipped to their children. We would come home with Jason's plastic pumpkin overflowing with full-sized candy bars, gingerbread ghosts and witches, carameled apples and homemade popcorn balls. I, the daughter-come-home, would be loaded down with packages of steak and hamburger as my parents' friends cleaned out their freezers before the men came home, and Ada Schmer would send us home with a dozen of her prized eggs, the ones with two and sometimes three deep-orange yolks inside which Jason consumed over-easy for breakfast.

We had had our parallel hunt of sorts, and back at my parents' house, we sat around and told our own stories, examined our own harvest, took pictures with our trophies. This quiet lull in our lives would last anywhere from three to five days before the men came home smelling gamier than the game itself, their collective mood broadcasting their success or failure.

One night we had all gone to bed, my parents, Jason, and I. The whole house was dark and quiet, when we were suddenly awakened by someone banging at the front door. My father, then in his sixties, hurried out of bed to see what was happening. My mother was right behind him. I lay in my bed upstairs, listening. I heard my father open the door. I recognized Stan's voice, excited, then my mother's, concerned. I looked at the clock. It flashed midnight. Before I could crawl from under the heavy quilts, Stan was in the room. He turned on the lights and pulled off the quilts.

"Get up!" he whispered excitedly. "C'mon, hurry!"

"What are you doing?" I mumbled, my brain still foggy.

"C'mon. Hurry and get dressed! You've got to come up on the mountain!" Stan added.

Before I could protest, he was down the stairs and back in the kitchen. I found him there, once I was dressed, rummaging through the refrigerator, my parents sitting at the kitchen table watching silently, refusing to become players in this midnight drama.

Stan stuffed a last bite of leftovers in his mouth and we were out the door. His father was waiting in the Ford Ranger, the motor running. It seems for all their good planning, they had miscalculated somewhere. Each blamed the other, but the irrefutable fact was that three, not two, elk--one bull and two cows--lay dead; there were only two, not three, hunters; and the game warden had been spotted on the mountain.

All the way up the mountain the two men, father and son, rehearsed me. I had to know how to shoot the gun. Crunched in between the two surly men, empty rifle pointed toward the far floorboard, I practiced working the bolt action back and forth, back and forth, until its glide was smooth, and I could feel the gun's pressure against my shoulder. My arm ached. It made me think of dance lessons in sixth grade music class, the awkward positioning of body to body, the artificial movements rehearsed, one-two, one-two, as I attempted to turn bolt action into glissando.

The two men coached me. I was to know the heft of the thing, not be caught off guard by its weight. I was to extend my left arm, cradle the barrel to support its girth.

"Keep it up, keep it up," one would say, "Don't let it dip."

"Keep it down," the other would say, "Here come some headlights!"

All the way up the mountain, I learned to say the words the men wanted to hear: hollow point, vent rib, recoil. I learned the serious nature of flirtation. I learned the glissando.

Just before daybreak, we saw dust on the road up ahead. The men, who had become more good-humored as they coached me, grew quiet. I felt my father-in-law grow tense. Stan placed the rifle back on the window rack. We strained our eyes into the approaching dust storm.

"If it's the warden, I'll do the talking," my father-in-law insisted.

As we neared the storm, we could see the light green of the game warden's truck.

"This is it. You're on," my father-in-law said quietly.

I could feel my pulse pounding in my temples. My body was honed. Is this what it's like, I wondered. Can he smell the fear racing wild through me?

The two trucks met in the middle of the road. Each rolled down a fogged-up window. Who would go first? Who was alpha, who beta?

"Spot anything?" my father-in-law ventured.

"No luck yet," the warden shot back, and as his eye lit on me, a pickup barreled over the top of the ridge, elk in the back, and almost ran smack into the back of the game warden's truck. My father-in-law shook his head, nodded at the warden, and drove off, leaving the warden to interrogate his newfound luck.

Once we arrived at camp, Stan and his dad set about their task. One bull, one cow were tagged and harvested. Legal tender. We talked in hushed voices. Wouldn't put it past him to circle back around. The third harvest was more problematic. I had to come along and carry a rifle. We walked a ways before Stan reached a gloved hand into the brush, began tearing out dead branches. Underneath the cover was a canvas tarp. Underneath the tarp lay a beautiful cow elk, her large brown eyes glassy as the lake top and just as impenetrable.

"She's yours," Stan said to me. "She's your first kill."

I found myself wondering, if this was my first kill, how many more did I have inside me? How many more until I was done? Would it get easier? But this hadn't been hard. Did I not even have to pull the trigger to be responsible? How many had my father killed before he was done? Did he feel guilt or shame? For a fleeting moment there, caught in the warden's gaze, I had felt game. I had tasted the pheromone of fear. Was I prey or predator? Guilt and shame did not figure in. I was game.

LA ESPERANZA

It is Christmastime. My birthday is three days away, and I am on the far side of middle age. There is the ugliest cup on campus sitting on my desk. What does it all mean?

I had been asked to reflect upon my journey, that perhaps I might shed light on a bit of wisdom waiting to be snapped up like some delectable crumb by a hungry reader. The idea intrigued me. *Hungry wolves on the prowl for scraps of knowledge, sniffing out the scent of understanding, hoping for a whole breastbone of wisdom.* We can be voracious in our appetites. This appetite—the hunger to learn.

As far back as I can remember I have been hungry to learn. A friend once described me as having *hambres atrasadas,* hungers following closely behind me, or as he described, a kind of "hunger nipping at my heels." It goes back, of course, to my parents: My father's and my early journeys scavenging the Wyoming badlands for fossils, arrowheads, and agates and the stories that accompanied them. I was a geologist at the age of four, gathering the most mundane rocks and pebbles to carry home to the garage where I would place them just so on the concrete, then deliver a blow of my hammer that would crack them wide open. Inside that dull exterior I might find a hidden world of crystals or expose a surface so new to light it glistened. At five, I was an anthropologist studying the tipi rings and medicine wheel tucked away in the Wyoming badlands. At six, I was Annie Oakley, sporting my leather-tooled holsters and matching silver pistols, riding high on my bucking, black, tire-swing stallion.

Then my mother, a fourth-grade teacher, took over. She brought home workbooks, flash cards, and *gold stars.* She confiscated from the elementary throw-aways a small school desk and filled the drawer with paper and pencils and a big box of crayons. I became a teacher. Every doll and stuffed elephant became my disciple. Today when I read articles about teaching apes to communicate, I think, *That's nothing. My animals were learning the alphabet when I was five.*

Now that I am older, I understand more clearly my parents' push for learning. I have seen firsthand the grove of trees down past the railroad tracks in that nearly forgotten southeast Kansas town. I have followed my father's gesture as he pointed precisely to the spot where his family's boxcar sat. I have heard loudly the message accompanying the silence that follows his memories. *What instructional pedagogy advises whacks with a ruler if a child has difficulty with vocabulary or syntax?* I can see in my mind's eye his mother, my grandmother, isolated by language and culture, in her boxcar kitchen mixing *masa* and patting out perfectly shaped tortillas. Her only companionship was the pride she felt in her children, especially in Francisco, *Pancho,* her eldest, who was excelling in school. I can see my grandmother come in late to the school Christmas pageant, slip silently into the back of the room and stand near the door for quick escape, in order to see her Pancho, dressed in his schoolmate's store-bought bathrobe—his shepherd's robe—lead the other, paler magi onto the small stage, his clear tenor voice ringing out across Bethlehem as he sang *en ingles*, "We Three Kings."

My grandmother, Maria Jesus Cortez de Sierra, died at the age of thirty-three. No one knows why for sure. It might have been a perforated stomach ulcer or perhaps, cancer. Being Mexican and poor, she had access to minimal medical care. My father, her pride and joy, was sixteen. It fell to him, then, to care for his three younger siblings while his father earned a living.

My mother's mother was a country schoolteacher herself, so when my mother received her diploma when I was in the sixth grade, it was already implanted in me that I came from a family of teachers. I resisted the idea of a foregone destiny for years. Teaching seemed so ordinary. A woman's profession, like hairdresser, or nanny.

It took me many years to discover the true value of teaching. I had a few things to learn before I would understand Robert Frost's words in *Two Tramps in Mud Time*: "My ambition is to unite my vocation and my avocation as my two eyes make one in sight." No matter what paths I pursued in life, certain hungers kept nipping at my heels. I might have been keeping the wolves at bay, much as my grandmother had by patting out tortillas, but ultimately, Education was inevitable. Learning was my destiny.

My journey took many turns before I landed at Kansas State University. First, I had a year-long stop at community college where I hit my first real bump of racism. I was an oboist. The school had purchased a brand new oboe just for me. I was passionate in my pursuit of the oboe. Until one day, that is. That was the day I arrived at practice, my horn together and warmed, the reed readied. I sat at attention on the edge of my chair, ready to make music. That was the day the director tapped his music stand with his baton and said, "Get out your *spic* music."

I could hardly believe my ears. This was not music! These tones made no harmony. I knew the word from somewhere, vaguely, but it had never been in my immediate proximity. Equally astonishing to me was that everyone seemed to understand the command! The members of the band began to rifle routinely through their music folders hunting for the Tijuana Brass. I was deeply wounded. I thought I was a valued part of the group. I thought I was among friends. The director never noticed. He raised his arms and the band responded. Good musical soldiers.

It was not business as usual for me, however. My arms wouldn't search through the folder. The reed refused to move to my lips. I sat there, captive to my own sense of justice, or was it my own budding sense of *self?* I had never felt different from my peers until that moment, but in that moment, surrounded by the bright sounds of the Tijuana Brass, I came to understand that I was indeed different. I felt as alienated as my grandmother Jesus. I could do nothing but pack up my oboe and escape out the door.

This was 1970, and I didn't know I could voice a complaint to anyone. So I went on with my classes, and I played my oboe, but from that day forward, I was someone new. My parents had prepared me for what I would one day encounter, not by warning me or dwelling on my difference. They had taught me that I must excel at whatever I valued. They had taught me without telling me not to allow others to label me.

At the end of that year, I ventured down a different path and over time found myself with a passel of new identities: military wife, mother, South-Sea-Island woman, auto salesclerk, sporting goods manager, student wife, veterinary receptionist. None of these new titles came with how-to books. Education took the form of trial-and-error adventure. I learned I could tolerate cockroaches when necessary. I discovered I liked squid. I could talk auto parts and fish bait. I could edit term papers and calm frightened dogs to passivity. As much as I liked motherhood and seeing my family prosper, I began to feel a void that my family could not fill.

One summer afternoon after work, a bunch of us drove up into the Wyoming mountains for a cook-out and some relaxation. I was sitting on a rock near a stream letting my mind wander when I saw a large fern, almost three feet tall, move erratically. The breeze was minimal, yet this fern was shaking. Then it stopped. I began to think I had imagined it when the fern began to tremble and then suddenly, it got shorter! I called to the others, and we watched this fern until over time, it had all but disappeared into the ground. Finally, one among us reached over and grabbed what was left of the fern. It gave no resistance. It came easily from the ground, no roots, no leaves left. Some unknown animal underground had satisfied its hunger.

The cook-out turned its attentions to hamburgers and chips, but I could not forget how quickly this tall, healthy fern had simply disappeared. It haunted me. I began to realize I felt just like the fern, as though I were caught in the undertow of someone else's hungers. I knew I had to make some changes. I had to feed my *Self*.

I decided I would enroll at Kansas State University for fall classes. I went to see an advisor who told me how to go about the process: "Whatever you do," he said, "don't start out by taking a class from Dr. Norma Bunton." He went on to explain that she would be far too demanding and intimidating in her expectations for me, a non-traditional novice.

I left his office feeling rather overwhelmed. I had been told to go fill out a FAFSA (whatever that was), to see the Registrar about my transcripts (*Registrar?*), to talk with an admissions representative, and when all that was accomplished, get in the lines for class selection but get there early as classes fill fast. I decided college was not for me: *I didn't even understand these basic directions!* I went home and did nothing.

Summer came to a close, and on the first day of classes I suddenly found myself longing to be a part of it all. I wanted just one class to see if I had the capacity to learn. I went back to the advisor who was less than pleased to hear that I had done nothing he had advised me to do. A few phone calls later, however, I was officially a Kansas State student. The advisor immediately enrolled me in Dr. Norma Bunton's Intro to Rhetoric class. *What was rhetoric?* I wondered.

Norma Bunton was the first woman department head at Kansas State University. She had served in World War Two and had a medal to prove it. She was tall, straight-backed, silver-haired, and had a no-nonsense air about her. Dr. Bunton took no guff. She became my professor, my mentor, and ultimately, my best friend. She nurtured and encouraged me. She praised and pushed me. She cajoled and scolded me. She taught me to think; she taught me to make a good martini. She believed in me, and more importantly, she made me believe in myself. She fed my *hambres atrasadas*.

A few years down the road I found myself telling students that there are many roads that lead to a destination. It may not be a truism that the shortest distance between two points is the fastest route. Paradoxically, the longer, more twisted road, the one with side paths and brambles and unexpected limbs blocking the way, may be the better route toward knowledge and wisdom. My young students did not always understand there was no one path to follow.

I was working in a program for high-achieving, serious-minded students who were, for the most part, first-generation college students, some inner city, many from families who had immigrated here in the last ten years. *The wolves are nipping at their heels.* I got to know their stories. There were stories of meat-packing plants, of cutting carcasses six days a week, stories of humiliation (the boss who calls everyone *Maria* or *Juan*). Families were divided, some sent to *el Norte* to live with an uncle and go to school, some left in Mexico too old for the trip.

What happens to the children? This is a question for our legislators, I am told, but to me, there is no question. The answer is apparent. The so-called *problem* is transparent. People need to have access to knowledge. Without education, people cannot contribute to their fullest potential. And who, in the deepest well within, does not have Hope? As long as Hope exists, human potential exists. It is when Hope dies that Despair moves in. And Despair can ruin the neighborhood.

Just before the holiday break, a student came to see me. He was a young man of few words. He was a thinker. He was a reader. He was a second-language learner. He made "A's" though no one would know it from his lips. He was Phi Kappa Phi. He wanted to work in a health field, probably become a doctor, in order to help his family and community. He had seen the back-breaking work that leads to health problems. He knew that being poor and minority was bad enough, but being poor, minority, *and* immigrant can limit one's opportunities even more. Knowing this, he applied the other fact he knew: *Education is the Equalizer.*

He didn't know this yet from experience. He knew it intuitively. He had read that knowledge is power. He had heard it. He wanted to believe it. And so he came to me. Without knowing my own story, he came intuitively, seeking that which Dr. Bunton gave to me some years ago. He came seeking encouragement. He came seeking hope. He did not know that Dr. Bunton gave me that ugly cup sitting on my desk: SECRETARY, it proclaimed in brash reds and yellow, once filled with Secretary's Day flowers. I kept it at first as a reminder that some day I would have a secretary instead of being one. I had kept it to remind me how to treat others, how to be a good mentor. Norma Bunton had stuffed that cup with blossoming Hope.

As I said, my student came to see me before he left for the holidays.

"I have something for you," he said.

He handed me a drawing in a frame. There on a stark black background sits a young girl. Her black hair is neatly combed. She wears a simple blouse and sits with her arms resting on a table top, a desk perhaps. Her face is serious, her eyes gaze intently into the darkness. A pencil is in her right hand, poised.

"I made it for your wall," he said simply.

Later, on email I asked him what the drawing should be titled and what the girl's name was. She had such presence there on the wall of my office that I felt the need to call her by name.

"Ms. Cortez," he wrote back to me, "I think her name should be *Esperanza*, but the drawing should be titled *Nuestra Esperanza*. Thank you for *la esperanza* that you give us all to be successful as students and as a people."

How do I tell him that it is he who has given a gift to me, that in fact, *La Esperanza* existed long before me. She lived in that boxcar. She lived with my grandmother as she watched her son sing *en ingles*. She lives in the meat-packing plants now, but more and more often these days, she is seen around the University. *La Esperanza* is pacing the halls of academe. Her pencil is writing on the walls.

TIME TRAVELERS

My education started the day I was born when my father took me in his arms and rested me on his shoulder where, clinging like a little sea creature new to this world, I began to survey this land.

My father was born in Morelia, Michoacán, Mexico, on October 4, 1917 (a year notable for revolution), the eldest son of a campesino who was less interested in the political tug-o-wars of Mexico than he was in dreaming big dreams born of desperation and a kind of stubborn optimism that would not give way to the more prevalent fatalism of his culture. Armed with optimism, my grandfather headed north with his small family, somehow believing he, Julio Cortez, could beat the odds, could avoid the Federales, could avoid the Revolucionarios and cross the Rio Grande successfully swaddled in darkness, with a wife, sick and silent with terror, a small infant straining at her breast.

Julio could hope and wait no longer, and in his eagerness to get on with it, he made a near-fatal error. One night, while making arrangements to leave his home, to leave the little village with its winding stone walls, the zocalo where evenings, young men strummed their homemade guitarros and young women with ribbons braided into their hair paraded arm-in-arm, whispering, giggling, hoping, waiting, he was waylaid. No one knows what error he made, but someone wanted him to pay. Julio was hanged by the neck from a tree branch and was left to linger in the consequences.

Julio's patron saint was with him that night, and I do not know by what miracle he survived his lynching, whether the knot slipped or the branch broke, or someone slipped from behind the brush, but my grandfather would not be deterred from his journey. Soon, his little family boarded a train headed north.

Crossing the border proved the least of their worries. Revolucionarios ambushed the train, looking for whom or what, I do not know. The bandits were full of machismo and their ideals. Armed and angry, they shot up the train, shattering windows and dreams, as politics and peasants crashed to the floor. Jesus, my grandmother, quickly laid her hungry baby on the cold, rough floorboards. Then she lay her own body down over the baby, my father, stifling his cries, nearly stealing his breath, that they might go undetected.

Miraculously, she was not shot. The bullets whistled over her as she lay still and silent. The baby under her knew of nothing but her protective warmth, her solidity, her scent of tobacco and masa and long labor, did not know the wails of others or the sting of bullets in the air; instead, he heard the *whooosh* of engine, the chug, the clank; he felt the vibration of wheel on track syncopated with his mother's heartbeat. The floorboards marked time until, with a shudder and a quake, the train started up, began to hobble northward.

They arrived safely in the United States where my grandfather found work, first in Texas, and eventually in Kansas where, like many Mexicans seeking their American Dream, he helped build the railroad tracks. Kansas would become home to my father, his siblings and their parents. Half a boxcar defined their piece of the pie. Kansas would be where, at the age of sixteen, my father would see his mother buried, as I mentioned, a victim of poverty and a perforated ulcer or perhaps, cancer. As eldest child, he assumed her duties. He cared for his father and three younger siblings, continued in school, became a hotshot guard on the Benedict basketball team, and eventually met, and fell in love with my mother, Emma Grace Usher, an Anglo--an Irish-English, Methodist, Republican, Kansas farm kid, a girl with spunk, who preferred basketball to ballet and played the banjo to boot, who wasn't above sneaking off for a swim or a movie, who wasn't afraid to define her own principles and defy the times by eloping to Wyoming to marry my father.

Railroading was in my father's blood, it seemed, siphoned from that first fateful train ride, and he made a career with the railroad. He went to telegrapher's school and landed an office job. He and his wife had three daughters and bought a house followed by a larger house and some land on the outskirts of town. Julio's dream had been realized. My father's family had made it.

It was in this larger house where I grew up. I grew up in the American Dream. We lived up on the bluff above town, across the river. It was called *the Heights,* and the families on the Heights had jobs in town but maybe owned a horse or raised some chickens or ducks.

My mother, always a woman ahead of her time, went back to school, got her teaching certificate and got a job teaching fourth grade in a neighboring town. Some neighbors and acquaintances undoubtedly questioned her decision--children at home to be raised, et cetera. But my mother was too bright, too energetic, to sit around home nibbling resentments with the other wives.

My father was my kindergarten. I remember the many mornings when, after my mother left for school, he would take me wandering the badlands in his '32 Chevy pick-up truck with its "AH-OOGA" horn that embarrassed my older sisters. It was these wanderings that taught me how to notice things, how to distinguish rattle of grasshopper from snake, how to translate what I saw, and how to respect. I learned to hunt. We scoured the sides of the hills like beetles scouring the seabed of history: gullies of grapheus, trilobites, ammonites--all yolks of petrified beginnings--agates, gizzard stones galore, worried to a permanent polish, the polished pebbles of life forms long perished.

When I tired, my father carried me piggy-backed upon his shoulders. He had a whole world hidden away in the hills among the sagebrush, down gullies. He had a forest: trees turned to stone, now stumps, and one long trunk lying as it fell millions of years ago, spread out in the dust, a lifeline for me to touch. He showed me where the buffalo had run over the bluff and landed in a big heap below. We would go there and dig in the sandy ground, sift out the bones. I found a whole horn there once, and my father told me how it had happened, painting a picture of the Indians and their survival. He showed me how the horn would be put to use, how every part of the animal was used, and how the whole camp would celebrate the hunt.

As soon as my mother was out the door to school, my father would say, "Go get your hat!" (She did not approve of our excursions because invariably the old truck would break down, get stuck in the ruts, or run out of gas--the gauge hadn't worked in years--and my father and I would hitchhike home, me perched like a sentinel on his shoulders, and he, late for work.) But when he called to me, I knew exactly what he meant. I would grab my red felt cowgirl hat and pull on my cowboy boots (protection against snakes and prickly cactus). While I gathered my mother's large, old handbag, which was now my treasure bag, my father would make our lunches--peanut butter and jelly and kool-aid. He would load pick-ax, shovel, canteen into the back of the truck. He never had to give me instructions. It was ritual. We'd climb in, and after coaxing the old truck a bit, off we'd start with a jerk or a sputter and a backfire or two.

This particular day, we headed toward Sheep Mountain, a sacred place, to scour the gullies below. My father would tell me how these Wyoming badlands used to be ocean, then showed me how the sandstone was worn from the lapping of ancient waters. We collected clam and oyster shells, grapheus and belemites; from our trips to the library, I knew these bullet-shaped fossils had once been squid-like creatures, soft-bodied and tentacled. We peered into the havens of black-widow spiders, tucked into the crevices of the ravine. I learned to recognize their glossy round bodies, the bright red hourglass. I learned not to fear but to respect. We were the intruders here. We looked, then left.

We came to a place where the Indians had camped. My father explained that we were time travelers. Millions of years had passed since we left the house that morning. We had dipped into the ocean, explored its floor, then moved on to the high plains where the Indians gathered near the sacred place. He showed me where there were still visible signs of the tipi rings, certain placement of stones. He showed me the center of the ring, told me to dig, and as I dug in the sandy earth, he told me how the fire was built in the center of the tipi, how as the smoke was drawn upward, the tipi warmed.

I kept on digging, but I am no longer sure what were his words, what were my imaginings. I only know that as I dug, my fingers felt warmed and the deeper I dug, the blacker the sand became. Soon my fingernails were charred by the sand. I had hit fire! I dipped my hands in and came up holding palmsful of black embers, the very embers that had warmed some other people before me. I could see the fire glow lighting the insides of buffalo hides, shutting out the howl of the Wyoming wind. I could see other brown hands reaching toward the heat, little hands like my own, and I could hear voices telling stories, stories about the *People*, stories about the land, stories about the spirits. My father and I were connected to them, connected in time, by place, and it all mattered. It was the mid-1950s and I was five years old, but my father was showing me that I, we, paradoxically, were much older and mere infants all at the same time.

After I had deposited the ash back in the circle of fire, I covered it again with the sand I had removed. I patted the earth down as though tamping the fire, brushed my hands on my blue jeans, and followed my father, who was slowly and silently approaching the Medicine Wheel. When I caught up to him, I reached out for his hand. There seemed some undefined force there, and I felt the need to be anchored in the reality of "Father." He took my hand and led me around the Wheel, pointing out the twelve spokes, their alignment with the sun, the seasons, the small cairns, perhaps for offerings.

"Who made the wheel?" I wanted to know, but my father remained silent, like the spokes themselves, all answers lost, unspoken in time.

"Would you like your lunch now?" he offered. He dug into the paper bag and brought out two peanut butter and jelly sandwiches. I was famished. I started to sit on the spoke of the Wheel, but he stopped me. "Don't sit there," he said. "Come sit over here and look at how far you can see." I gnawed on my sandwich and gazed off in the distance, happy, and somehow knowing there was nowhere else on Earth I would rather be. My father gave me a chug of kool-aid from the thermos. I knew I was, at that moment, blessed.

As I finished my sandwich, I made circles in the dust with the tip of my boot. Who remembers what children dream in such moments of utter contentment? I had ceased to be a creature of cognition. I was like the blue-bellied lizard sunning itself on the lichen-covered granite, just creature, nothing more, fulfilling my need for nourishment. As my boot moved in its diurnal swing, a glimpse of color caught my eye in the dust. I leaned over, closer to the ground; I saw nothing. I slid off my rock and with my hand began to filter the sand through my fingers. At first, I saw nothing, but then I saw it. There it was, catching the light in my hand. A green bead. Old. Dull. Minuscule. But somehow, illuminated. I ran to show my father. He studied it. Yes, he said, it was old, very old, had, in fact, probably come from a moccasin.

"A moccasin? Really? A moccasin?" I repeated. "Yes, a moccasin," he said. "Let me put it in my wallet so you don't lose it before we get home."

I obligingly handed over my treasure.

"Yes," he continued, "this bead must have quite a history to it." And he proceeded to tell me about the history of the bead. He painted pictures of the Shoshone, of the Blackfoot, the Sioux, and traders, and trappers. He spoke of food and glittery goods and guns and furs. He spoke of music and storytelling, of dancing and fighting. And he spoke of a woman named Sacajawea. He told how Sacajawea had endured many hardships, how she had led Lewis and Clark from St. Louis to the West Coast, led them there safely, fording rivers, climbing mountains, meeting Indians, and being a mother.

When she wasn't preparing food, making buffalo-hide boats, or acting as interpreter, she was sewing clothing. But the one thing she most loved was making moccasins for her baby. She had saved the most beautiful beads for her baby's shoes, and this green bead was one of them. Oh, it used to be much brighter and greener but just think how bright it must have been to still hold on to its green-ness now all these years later. Sacajawea probably had a whole pouch of green beads as well as white and yellow and blue and red ones. But the green were her favorite because they captured the spring and all the promise that it holds. And so she had covered her baby's moccasins with green, with promises, each bead representing a wish for her infant.

But one bead had come loose. In all the climbing and roaming and struggling, one bead had worked its way free of the moccasin, had fallen near the Medicine Wheel where she knelt with her baby on her back, while she sought the voices of the elders, of the spirits who could lead her and her entourage safely across the Rockies. The bead was meant to fall there. It was an offering exacted by the spirits--one promise, one wish denied her baby in order that some other child hence could stumble across it, could pick up the promise and hear it speak.

And so I gave it to my father to hold safe for me.

Later, when my mother returned home from school, I eagerly told her of my find. As I told the story, my father dug into his wallet to bring out the bead, but the bead was gone. My father continued searching the wallet and his pockets. He had lost my bead. He had been so sure it would be safer with him than with me. He was mortified. But I had other things to do. I had told my story. Now it was time to check out my many haunts around the property. I was done with the bead.

Many years later, my parents came to visit my family, and as we were reminiscing about days gone by, I remembered the wanderings of my father and me.

"Daddy," I said, "remember that green bead...."

But before I could continue, my ordinarily quiet father broke in: "I don't know what happened," he said. "I put it in my wallet. I put it in the coin purse so it couldn't get lost, and I didn't open the wallet until we got home to show your mother. I put my wallet in my pocket and I checked my pockets too, but it wasn't there. I don't know what happened. I don't know how I could have lost that bead."

And as he continued, I ceased to hear him. I was remembering that day, the bead, its green glint in the dust those many years before. I was remembering the treasure I held in the palm of my hand, those wanderings with my father, the steep, bumpy paths over trails where buffalo-hunters had once passed.

BIRD SEASON

It was bird season again. It comes around like clockwork. All the men get itchy. They start getting their gear together. They oil their weapons. Their stories turn toward their aim. Their adrenaline pumps. The birds, like motley green mallards, fly in formation taking off over the pond. Three B-52s take off over the South Sea Island cliffs of Tarague Beach, three come home to roost. We are at war. Clockwork.

The war in Viet Nam is in its big build-up. It is the year before the end, 1972. It is before we all know that Nixon is a crook. I am twenty-one years old, living in the midst of tent cities crawling with men. I am a young wife, a mother, an ex-prom queen who thought all South Sea Islands were paradise.

Guam had been in many ways a year-long holiday on a south sea island for me. Amidst the thickets of jungle (Guam was said to have the world's thickest jungle), there were green canvas tents everywhere--tent cities where many of the enlisted G.I.s lived. And I have to admit, the day my son and I arrived at five-thirty in the morning in early June, Guam looked more like the last earthly outpost than an island for a romantic interlude.

We had been traveling for seventeen hours. It was my first trip alone without a parent or husband to take care of me, and now I was responsible not only for myself but for my toddler as well.

The light was just breaking, muggy and diffuse. The air was thick and smelled of sea salt, blossoms and garlic. Sounds of language, unfamiliar in tone, accents and rolls, all mixed together in this international stew pot where even the English I heard sounded foreign.

This airport seemed scarcely bigger than the one I had left behind in Wyoming. In fact, this airport did not even have a pay phone. There was one public phone which, judging from people's frustration, seemed to reach no one, yet everyone wanted to call someone. It seemed that every traveler who had the ill fortune to be stranded here had the good fortune to know someone to call.

I had envisioned the scene of our arrival. *My handsome husband would be there in his dress blues, pacing and checking his watch, eager and impatient. He would swoop us up into his arms the moment we stepped from the plane, and from that moment forward all my worries would be over in this Paradise of Plenty. Stan would hunt fish, deer and wild boar while I picked bananas and papaya. Jason would grow chubby on coconut milk. Our condo would be light and airy and we would sun ourselves like lazy lizards in the afternoons on something called the "lanai," one of those exotic-sounding words I had only encountered in books. Would we have a maid, I wondered?*

Around me, all was exotica. Beaches, palm trees, tan young men, and sunrise splattered blood red across the horizon. Paradise. But even paradise is not perfect.

When Stan did arrive, I did not recognize him as he approached; it was Jason, my toddler genius, who held out his arms to this tanner, trimmer version of a man I had once known. This man was not in starched dress blues. He was not spit-polished. He was dressed in green fatigues, damp and rumpled from a night in the jungle. He had five o'clock shadow and smelled faintly of his guard dog as he embraced me.

"What are you doing here?" he greeted me, already looking past me to Jason who was eager to jump into his embrace.

Ensconced in our new car, a 1964 red Rambler, the paint appropriately faded to match the rust, we headed to our new home. Jason was fascinated with the holes Stan had drilled in the floor boards of the car to let the rain run through. Jason could watch the coral bump by as we drove. As he remained riveted to the floor of the car, I took in the scene around me. Roads were a skeletal white, powdered with a red dust that was made of coral. Creeping up to the very edges of the road were green fingers of vines. G.I.s were everywhere one looked. In fact, coming in to land, there had been so many that, when I looked down, they appeared as ants scurrying over everything, busily serving their queen, Lady Liberty. The locals, on the other hand, seemed less harried. I was surprised as we drove along at how many people of Hispanic descent I saw. Mailboxes had names like Guitierrez, Rodriguez, Benevides.

They look like me, I thought happily, and indeed, the influence of early Spanish explorers was everywhere in the stone walls and bridges, in the features of Guamanians, and as I later learned, in the soft sounds of spoken Chamorro, in the love of spicy foods, in the importance of family.

Home turned out to be four rooms in a condemned cinder-block house in Dededo. As we pulled up to the house, the stench of baby vomit in the air was overwhelming. It was not Jason. It was the rotting papayas that littered the ground around the only entrance to the house. I held my breath and stepped carefully over the slime of rot and feasting snails as I warded off the question, *This is my new life?*

As Stan held open the torn screen door for me to enter, Jason pointed upward. I looked up just in time to see a lizard hanging by his tail from the doorframe.

"That," Stan offered, "is a sign of good luck. That is a gecko, and every house has them. They are like house pets here."

House pets, I thought. House pests. Paradise has house pests.

But here I was. I was a twenty-one-year-old ex-prom queen from Greybull, Wyoming. I was National Honor Society, first oboist in the All-State Band for three years running. Honors This and Honors That. Voted Best Dressed in the Senior Yearbook. Only kid in my class who had been to Europe. Miss Blessed. Miss Silverspoon-in-Her-Mouth. Miss Most-Imagined. Miss Reality: Miss Dropped-Out-of-College-to-Marry-the-Football-Star. Miss Pregnant-at-Nineteen. Ms. Mom. I had been traveling for seventeen hours.

There was simply no housing available anywhere on Guam. This was the time of the great build-up of troops for Viet Nam and every available bed was occupied, thus the huge tent cities scattered like so much sea debris on the island, the G.I.s' drunken hollers like predatory seagulls. Stan had been forced by my impending, somewhat ill-advised arrival to drive the back roads, stopping at every quonset hut to ask where he might find a place. Finally he got lucky. Someone had a friend who had an uncle who knew someone who. . . .

The deal was struck under the table. A condemned hut. Pay in cash. Don't ask for anything other than what's there. *As is.* Two hundred six bucks a month, two hundred and six bucks non-refundable deposit. Don't tell people where you are living. Don't bother the landlord. *Oh, but here's a puppy for your boy there. Boy needs a dog. Pup's mother was a damn good ratter. Doberman-terrier mix. Haf Adai!*

And that was our lease to one half of a condemned cinder-block building with a torn screen door and a rusty latch hook. Ducking under the gecko as I passed through the doorway, I entered the kitchen. It consisted of a stove, refrigerator, and an enameled sink the texture of gray granite from years of embedded filth.

When Stan left for work, I went to bed, but I could not sleep. I sat up all night, unwilling to close my eyes. I sat in the kitchen in the dark in one of the rickety straight back chairs where I could keep an eye on the torn screen door. There, with nothing but moonlight filtering through the louvered windows, I wrote a letter home:

Dear Mother and Daddy, Greetings from my little slice of Paradise. Stan is at work, Jason is asleep, so I am basking here in the moonlight coming through the window. Things are going well.

My eye caught a movement by the stove. There in the crack of the stove swung a tiny, helpless gecko, its head stuck, its body swinging and flailing. I began to jot on a fresh piece of paper what was to become, years later, this primary memory:

Four A.M. in Dededo, Guam

Air like sticky syrup
too thick to drip clogs the sounds
of the jungle. Some skeletal mutt
howls, prowling for food. Nothing
between me and that scavenger's search
but a torn screen and a rusty latch hook.

Three B-52s take off for Nam.
Where are the ukeleles, the South Sea Island breeze?
I stick my lower lip out and blow.
A strand of hair clutches my brow, clings.
My flashlight scans the stove for the time.
All it finds is a gecko, its head
caught in a crack in the stove, helpless.

Stan's work schedule was such that he worked four nights on and three nights off. I looked forward to his off days because he was my only companionship.

We all loved the beach. Jason shoveled sand and dumped Tonka trucksful into the ocean. He excavated the beach. He gathered bucketsful of hermit crabs, then dumped them unceremoniously to watch them scamper toward the water for cover. Who knows what is inside little boys? Why did he suddenly have an undeniable urge to dump a bucket of hermit crabs on the bare belly of a woman sunbathing nearby? And what male charm did he exude that brought the woman to her knees to teach him the fine art of castle building there in the sand?

As Jason labored over castles and kingdoms of crabs, I lay basking on my blanket, letting the sun come down on me, rolling this way and that to accommodate its touch. I lay listening to the ebb and flow, watching the white gulls dip and swoop against blue. I felt the tidal tug within, the scent of salt in my nostrils. I could taste my own desire.

Overhead, a short distance away to the north, the B-52 bombers insinuated their power over this land, this sea, these peoples, three every three minutes. They were more interesting to watch than the commercial jets with their wispy white contrails etch-a-sketched across the sky.

The B-52s were close enough to be real. I could see their motley colors. Their rumbling shook the air. They took off methodically, rhythmically. Three would take flight over the reef, one after the other without faltering. Three would come settling down over the rocks to the west. Occasionally before landing, one would drop its leftover cargo like a rotten egg into the ocean beyond the reef. The sound of bombs bursting would singe the air, the spray of saltwater sizzle. I felt a sort of connectedness with the scheme of things.

Stan emerged flipper-footed from the ocean, slumped under the weight of tanks and spear-gun, mask marks on his forehead. We were ready to return home. I looked forward to a cool shower.

After Stan had inspected the shower for water bugs, I stripped and stepped under the stream of water. I winced in pain. I looked down at my legs. They were lobster red. Even under the cool stream of water my skin felt hot. My veins glowed. I felt nauseous and dizzy. I looked Jason over. He was brown but not red.

I lay on the bed naked because anything touching my body hurt. I couldn't move. I drifted into sleep for a little while until I was startled awake by a sharp pin-prick on my stomach. A fly had landed on me. It felt like a hat pin had been driven into my gut.

I learned to endure an over-sized T-shirt of Stan's as well as my humiliation. I was branded *New Mainlander*. As my burn turned from blisters to brown and as I began to take on the shade of islander, I learned to spot every newcomer by the shade of his skin. Indeed, as the year wore on, the shade of my skin became a source of pride to me. Guam was such a melting pot of people from all over the world that I could pass for most anything I chose. Guamanians thought I was Guamanian. Hawaiians thought I was Hawaiian. Italians claimed me. A Black man told me I looked just like his sister back home.

Being a woman on Guam was perplexing. There were too many lonely, scared G.I.s there at the Air Force Base and Navy Base, not to mention the tent cities that housed young men for the Viet Nam build-up between 1972 and 1973. It was confusing. I had managed to get a job as a salesclerk at the Base Exchange, so I met almost every G.I. who passed through Guam.

(Looking back now, I don't know what saved me. My own naïveté? Perhaps the only thing I internalized from my short stint of Catholicism was a strong sense of guilt.) I watched many a marriage go bad that year. I watched Minnie, a fifty-five-year-old grandmother with a pot-belly and receding chin, be transformed by a forty-five-year-old family man (whose family was in Ohio). I watched her hair turn red, her lips pink. I watched her step lighten, her eyes waken. I watched the family man watch me.

I watched another woman with three adorable boys, all under five, fidget nervously when her handsome husband came by. I noticed her frequent absence when a certain security guard was making his rounds. And no one seemed shocked, or even mildly disapproving, when she ran off with the guard, leaving her husband the boys. It seemed inevitable. Too many men. Not enough women.

When I was in high school, it was considered patriotic for young women to write letters to the young men in Viet Nam, whether we knew them or not. My parents were protective of me, and I was never allowed to associate with anyone they did not know, but when it came to soldiers in Viet Nam, I was allowed to write. My sister Eloise was in the Women's Army Corps at the time, so she had given me the address of a soldier named Tony, who was from Hawaii. Terry, the boy next door, the closest thing I had to a brother, joined the Marines, so I wrote to him. One day I received a letter, along with a photograph, from a soldier named Richard. He was from Texas but had seen my picture in the local paper of one of his bunkmates, so I wrote to him. My parents voiced no disapproval, until the day Richard wrote that he was coming home and would be coming to see me first thing.

By this time, he imagined he was quite in love with me. It was a major dilemma. How should I tell my parents? How could I tell Stan, already my boyfriend by then? I wanted to meet Richard. He was handsome and his letters charming and full of imagination. I wanted our correspondence to go on and on, an imaginary relationship.

I finally dropped the bomb Richard had avoided in Nam. I did not want him to come to Wyoming. My parents would not let me see him. I had a boyfriend. He was home safe and sound. Our relationship was over.

But the war was not over. Only Richard's war was over. For me, the war hadn't even started. Viet Nam did not fully come home to me until I lived on Guam, until I met all those G.I.s, watched all those B-52s fly overhead, watched those marriages collapse. The war didn't come home to me, in fact, for years. Or, to be truthful, it may never come home to me. War is something I had to experience from a distance, being woman, being American woman. I would only experience it in light of the men in my life. I would experience it only through cleaning up, in trying to bring order.

I met many men at the Base Exchange. It was the center of their social life. Most of the sales staff were female. There was always music playing. (The Exchange sold massive stereo components from Japan at ridiculously low prices.) Two of the favorite songs that year--Roberta Flack's *Killing Me Softly* and another song I have never heard on the Mainland, *My Ding-a-Ling* --constantly rang through the aisles. Every woman salesclerk, young or middle-aged, had her own following of soldiers. I had mine too. There was a sense in which we all knew that part of our job was to boost their morale. None wanted to be here on Guam. Many were sent "TDY" (temporary duty) over and over. This meant that they could not bring their families.

Many were "fly boys" who were making bombing missions or piloting fighter planes. Each time they left the island, they did not know whether they would be back. This came home to me one bright sunny day when an unfamiliar soldier came to pick up the film of one of the G.I.s. This G.I., a follower of mine, was a major. He was attractive, tall, blond and blue-eyed. He used to come talk to me between missions. So when a strange colonel came to pick up his film, I coyly asked why he was running such errands for a major. Instead of the usual flirtation I expected, he informed me that the major had been shot down, was dead.

I was stunned. This did not happen in my world. My world was handsome, tanned young men and innocent flirtation. My world was *young*! People did not die in my world. And then they did.

One day Anderson Air Force Base held an open house for all the soldiers' families so that we might see and better appreciate what our spouses were up to. It was a social event. All the officers, or at least the officers' wives, would be there to greet the enlisted families. The flyboys who were not otherwise engaged would show up too, all starched and stiff and spit-polished. They would lead the tours, show off their own birds, even as they sized up their buddies' wives and the officers' daughters.

I wanted to see the birds. I had watched them so often, I felt as though I knew them, was in tune with them. The B-52s were big and sturdy, and I was fascinated with them. The flash and dazzle fighters with their shark-toothed grins had more pizzazz, but the B-52s possessed the real power. They just were. Lives depended upon their strength and endurance. The free world counted on them. They were America. They could deliver death, preserve life. And I--I was going to see them up close, touch one, maybe even enter one. *How many prom queens have been here*, I wondered.

I dressed for the occasion. It was important. Even the general was going to say a few words. This was like participating in heart surgery. This was the pulse of America, and we were part of the team. I wore a white cotton mini-dress, its hem a good seven inches above the knee, little puff sleeves, the tiniest pale yellow daisies outlining the bodice. Transparent net sandals on bronzed feet. Bare legs. Alabaster on bronze.

Next I dressed Jason. He was only two. I slipped his Air Force toddler T-shirt over his head, his navy-blue shorts over his Pampers. He began to jabber happily.

"We're going to see the birds," I said to him. "Do you want to see the great big birdies where Daddy works?"

"Birdie," Jason repeated, his little hand grabbing for sky. And we were off.

On the Tarmac the planes were lined up ceremoniously. Fighters lined the right side of the runway, their bodies sleek and shiny for the occasion. They reminded me of over-sized mosquitoes, pesky little insects with lethal bites. Some of the fly boys stood by their birds, feet slightly apart, arms folded across their chests, bodies arched slightly back. Erect. Shivers went up and down my spine.

"We are Americans," I chirped happily to Jason. He waved his little American flag, handed to him as we entered the gate, then cocked his chubby finger to shoot at seagulls overhead.

The microphones began to buzz. It was time to take a seat and hear what the General had to say. He was glad we could all be here today. He was proud to open the gates to Anderson Air Force Base, to show us *this great fleet of birds where America's day begins*. He was proud of the men who *kept us free and defended our families back home*. And for us ladies in the audience, he appreciated our contributions to his men as well. He hoped we would allow these fine men to introduce us to their world. They were *eager to show you what they can do, and ladies, these fine men do it better than any I know*.

Next, there was some platoon parade. Peacock strut stuff. Enlisted men. Stan would have been in this had he not been on duty. I hurried off with Jason toward the planes. At the end of the area, they had a C-5, its backend open, a gigantic piece of equipment exposed to show us its girth. The C-5s were the Clydesdales of the Air Force. Impressive in their way. But I was drawn to the birds of prey, the life-makers and takers, the B-52s.

I climbed up the steps into the middle bomber. As I approached the entrance, I hesitated for just a moment. Here I was on the verge of crossing over, but over into what? I had lain on the sandy beach of Tarague and watched perhaps this very plane, its belly heavy with bombs, fly over me. I had lain there, unconcerned with that other beach, with the other women and children who might be watching this same plane fly over, who might wish for nothing more than to look up into the sky and see a clear day dawn.

I gave my hand to the young captain, who flashed a welcoming smile and offered his assistance as I delivered my baby boy into the heart of the beast.

SITTING DUCKS

While the National Rifle Association and our state and national legislators debate our country's right to bear arms and our right to carry assault weapons, a small society of hunters goes about unaffected, unchecked and unnoticed by all concerned. They are under the radar, as the saying goes. They have traded clay pigeons for feathered ones, guns for falcons. They have turned fowl to foul.

The peregrine is the most prized among the birds of prey. They are thought to be the fastest animal in the world, capable of diving at speeds up to 200 kilometers, deadly accurate, beautiful and in many areas, still endangered. A person must have a license to have a peregrine in his possession. Such licenses are limited to those who can care for injured raptors, usually men in Fish and Wildlife or veterinarians who specialize in raptors. There are so few in this special society that they know each other all across the country if not the globe. They will travel through several states to help each other out, to arrange a hunt, to bring an injured bird for treatment. All other work comes to a standstill while the peregrine reigns supreme.

When they get together, the stories tend toward the exotic. One man might have stories about his travels in Dubai, Saudi Arabia, or bustard hunting in Pakistan. Another might share how the sheiks pack huge trucks full of expansive tents, hand-woven carpets, furniture and beds, cooking stoves and the gas to heat them, generators for refrigeration and air conditioning for the tents. *And that was just for the falcons,* they like to joke. Another might have a story about a sheik's bedroom, an homage to the bird, the bed itself nestled in huge falcon talons, a beautiful dark-haired woman reclining as though caught in the claws that held her. And then there were the young boys, leading their own private peregrines around on leashes as though they were puppies. Sometimes they would toss the birds into the air and pull them back gleefully as the bird tried to fly. Some sheiks tolerated their young sons' behaviors; others would not. It was a wise man, so the stories claimed, who knew which sheiks tolerated mistreatment, which did not.

Doug was a member in good standing of this society. He was the only veterinarian in several states licensed to rehabilitate raptors. Injured birds came to the clinic on a fairly regular basis, but often they were golden eagles, owls, an occasional hawk, a kestrel or two. Everyone at the clinic had been taught what and how to feed the birds. The technicians knew how to restrain them for treatment. The larger birds were so strong that once they began to regain their health, they had to be restrained by men. Few women had the strength to hold them down and still. Even so, everyone had a real respect for those beaks and talons.

One day the phone rang. It was a Fish and Game man from a northern state. He had come across an injured peregrine. He could *be at the clinic with the bird in eighteen hours. Would Doug be there?* The whole clinic atmosphere changed. Everyone was scurrying around. Dogs had to be fed and cages cleaned early so there would be free time in eighteen hours. Surgeries were moved up, back, or cancelled and rescheduled. The best cage was prepared for the falcon. Dinner plans needed to be made. That was Sharon's job. After the peregrine was attended to, the dinner party would begin, and the stories would flow along with the wine.

The peregrine would stay at the clinic until it was well enough to be moved to Doug's personal raptor house on his property. There the raptor would stay until it was fully recovered and strong enough to be released into the wild. If the weather was especially bad, say in January or February, a bird might spend the winter at Doug's "raptor resort." Such was the case with this particular raptor. It had recovered nicely. It was a young falcon and would be released into the wild in the spring. Meanwhile, it would eat well and wait out the winter.

Life at the clinic had turned back to its routine. Surgeries in the mornings, appointments in the afternoon, out the door by 5:30. Small talk in between appointments, weekend plans firmed up. Mid-winter was always more relaxed. Doug had a hip replacement on a St. Bernard that morning, in addition to several routine spays and neuters. That was the difference. Hip replacements almost always ran into the lunch hour. And he needed Stan to assist with the surgery. Stan was strong and in good shape. He could heft that dog around like it was a poodle. And if Doug's arm started to give out drilling through bone, Stan could take over. Doug's relief pitcher, so-to-speak.

Some days just seem destined to go bad from the start. The last thing Doug needed to come through the door when he was in the middle of hip surgery was a Doberman with an intestinal torsion. This meant his whole day would be spent in surgery, no doubt. No way would he be able to get away to look in on the falcon. He liked to do that over the lunch hour, living on the outskirts of town like he did. He never really expected any problem, but he just wasn't comfortable with that family next door, the only neighbors he had. What if that Pomeranian of theirs found a way into the raptor house, for instance?

He decided to send Sharon home to grab some lunch for him and to check on the birds. She knew how to observe the birds and tell whether they were feeling all right. She was familiar with their individual quirks. Doug resigned himself to a day of bones, blood, drills, and hammers.

Sharon went home looking forward to a long lunch to herself. She went to the bedroom and stripped off her clothes. She went to the closet and pulled down her swimsuit, a black one-piece, knowing as she did, ever since seeing *Psycho*, that a woman alone should never be naked. That thought made her giggle. She knew she was superstitious. Doug said she was. Even so, she hated to shower in an empty house. It made her think of knives. Knives had always made her nervous. She never left them out on the counter at bedtime; they were always tucked safely away and out of sight. She wondered if it went back to the time in her childhood when her parents were arguing in their upper Eastside apartment in New York. She didn't know what they were arguing about at the time, but now she thinks it must have been about her father's indiscretion. She remembers sitting at the dining table, mahogany polished to a mirrored surface. Her mother suddenly standing up from the table, saying something accusatory to her father. Her mother with a large carving knife in hand, chasing her father around and around the table while Sharon sat there pleading with her mother, *Don't kill him! Please don't kill him!*

She remembers her mother's reply to this day: "I'm not going to *kill* him," she said disdainfully, "I only want to *hurt* him. Do you think I would go to prison for this man?"

But today was her opportunity to luxuriate. She secretly lived for those days when Doug was held hostage at the clinic and she could escape for some rare time to herself. She went to the kitchen and grabbed a glass of chardonnay, some sourdough and brie, and a perfectly ripe pear, then headed for the hot tub. She leaned her head back, closed her eyes, drew the scent of the chardonnay deeply into her nostrils, and let the slightly warm water lap gently over her. Christopher Parkening serenaded her with his guitar. No dogs barking, no doors slamming shut, no men barking orders. Peace and quiet on a January day. Just as she was letting the cold wine ease down her throat, the schnauzer started barking and jumping at the window.

Sharon sat straight up almost choking as she swallowed. There in the yard was a strange vehicle with out-of-state tags. *Was it Texas? Who could it be*, she wondered. She went to the window and then she saw. A man, a rather large man, dressed in a man's brown insulated coveralls and a brown ski mask, was inside the raptor house.

"What are you doing in there?" Her voice didn't even sound like hers. It was high and shrill and she hadn't stopped to think before running out the door in her bathing suit in mid-January in Wyoming. She didn't know if she was shivering with fear or cold. The schnauzer barked from inside the heated hot tub room. It hadn't even tried to follow her outside. The falcons were keening in their high-pitched cries. The man paused to look directly at her. He reached inside his zippered coveralls and pulled out a gun and pointed it at her.

"Shut up," he said, "I don't want to use this thing."

Sharon was too frightened to respond. Her feeble inner voice had gone into hiding just like the damn schnauzer. She couldn't think what to do.

The man grabbed the rehabilitated falcon and stuffed it none too gently into a large shoe box. He shoved the box under his arm and shoved the gun hard into Sharon's ribs. She continued to tremble.

The man smiled. *"You're a right pretty lady, ma'am. Awful nice to see you in your bathing suit on a bright January day. Bet you'd look nice in your birthday suit too, wouldn't you, little lady?* He jabbed the gun harder into her ribs. *You get in this chicken coop, sweetie pie, and don't you come out until I have disappeared down the road, you understand?"*

Sharon nodded yes. She understood. The man looked her up and down, settled on her breasts, licked his lips, gave her one last jab, then turned toward his vehicle. He opened the trunk, lifted the carpeting and stashed the box containing the falcon where the spare tire should be. He got in the vehicle, waved his gun out the window, and headed down the road.

Sharon was chilled to the bone. She waited as long as she could see the vehicle on the road, then ran to the house. She grabbed a throw from the back of the couch and wrapped it around her. Still shaking with cold, fear, and fury, she dashed to the phone.

She dreaded giving the news to Doug. She knew how he would react. He would become obsessed with this thief. A healthy young falcon might bring $40,000 or more on the black market. Somehow, someone knew the falcon was recuperating here.

Doug was on the phone within seconds of Sharon's call. He called the local police, the sheriff, the highway patrol, the local Fish and Game, the state Fish and Game; he alerted all the veterinary clinics in the neighboring states, and he told all licensed falconers to be on the lookout for a suspiciously rumpled bird. He jumped in his Subaru and started patrolling the highway himself, looking for the description of the vehicle Sharon had given.

In spite of Sharon's fear and the fact that the man was covered from head to toe, Sharon had had time to look over the vehicle from the hot tub. To her own amazement, she was able to give an accurate description not only of the vehicle but the tags as well. By the second day of the hunt, the kidnapper was apprehended in the panhandle of Texas. The news was not all good, however. When they lifted the shoebox from the tire well, nothing but silence greeted them. The bird had succumbed to the trauma.

A young falcon was dead, a woman was traumatized, a man went to prison. For the men in this small society of falconers, though they did not know the poem, Yeats' words were confirmed: "Turning and Turning in the widening gyre/ The falcon cannot hear the falconer;/ Things fall apart; the centre cannot hold;/ Mere anarchy is loosed upon the world,..."

***

The day the phone call came, informing us that Stan had been accepted into veterinary school, we knew the long, crooked path that had led us there was worth it. The call came to the clinic where we both worked, he as a student-apprentice, I as a receptionist. Getting in was a long shot, we thought, since his early grades had been so abysmal and since he had admitted in his Colorado State University interview that he had smoked marijuana. That first rejection from Colorado was such a disappointment. I knew he had received the letter in the mail when I came home at noon and found a box of cereal, left on the kitchen table that morning, crushed as though a fist had smashed down upon it. We got used to the rejections after awhile, and finally, contented ourselves to think of alternate lives.

When I answered the clinic phone and was told the voice on the other end belonged to Dr. So-and-So from Kansas State University, I could do nothing but stammer for Stan. As Stan took the call, the rest of us in the clinic gathered around trying to gleen what we could from the one-sided conversation.

"Yes, sir. Thank you, sir. I certainly would, sir," was about the extent of Stan's side of the conversation, but when he hung up the phone, he announced his resignation effective the end of the summer. We floated through the rest of the afternoon.

That evening, Doug and his wife invited us to their house for dinner. They lived outside of town on a dirt road, and when we got there, Doug was just emerging from the pigeon coop.

"Come on," he said. "We need to fix you a drink to celebrate!"

We went into the kitchen where Sharon was busy working at the counter.

Doug opened the refrigerator, looked around in there for a bit and said, "Sharon, didn't you get some tonic when you were at the store?"

Sharon was the epitome of efficiency whereas Doug was more of a dreamer. She stopped chopping long enough to go to the refrigerator. She too stared at the cluttered mish-mash on the shelves. The refrigerator was packed solid--plastic bags of vegetables spilled out onto the floor, some crisp and green, some a fermented mush; there were containers with crusted lids; shrink-wrapped filet mignon, Perrier, and far to the back behind something white and fluffy were the bottles of tonic water.

"There it is," she said, "in the far corner."

"Aha!" Doug chortled. "Tanqueray and tonic coming right up!"

He reached in and instead of pulling out the tonic, he pulled out a pigeon, its head still attached. Its eyes stared unblinkingly, its beak slightly open as though frozen mid-gasp, its feathers scarcely ruffled.

"Rose's lime juice?" he asked.

He placed the pigeon on the butcher block while he hunted for the lime juice. The pigeon lay there, its neck slightly askew, its dark eyes staring dully. It smelled of damp feathers.

Doug must have noticed the look in my eyes because he laughed and said, "Oh--this isn't our dinner. It's for peregrine practice."

Our dinner was considerably more than pigeon. We had prime rib and to celebrate, a bottle of Rothschild Chateau Lafite,1972. Doug poured the wine and raised his glass to toast: "To the new doctor."

We were about to drink when he said, "Stop! Don't drink until I finish. To our futures--may they be entwined from this day forward. You do agree to come work for me when you are finished with school?"

We were flattered. Stan had just been accepted to veterinary school and already he had landed a good job! Doug was a good doctor, a brilliant surgeon. He was the best veterinarian in the state to repair discs. People brought their dachsunds from all across the state for back surgery. And the dachsunds went home healed but looking like little walking footballs, zippers the lengths of their backs, his signature surgery, we used to joke.

It was a heady evening. Our future was secured. We moved to the living room for chocolate mousse followed by tiny crystal glasses of amaretto. Out the window to the north, we could see the dusk was settling in. The bird calls quieted. Through the open window came the sounds of early summer evening: frogs from the meadow ponds, crickets, and an occasional coyote.

As I climbed into our 1973 Chevy Nova, I felt like Cinderella with the Prince, climbing into the pumpkin for the last time before it turned into a crystalline future. Our own castle was just a few short years away down this same dusty road.

For the next four years, we lived in Kansas through the fall, winter, and spring, but we always made the trek home to Wyoming for the summer. We would load up the bare essentials in the Ford Ranger pickup and Chevy Nova, along with everything living: one Star Wars-infested child, one alley cat we had rescued from the veterinarian's needle when its owner brought it into the clinic for euthanasia for eating her canary, one neurotic, naked cockatoo who had picked itself bare and would eat nothing voluntarily but bananas, one aquarium-raised cockatiel who whistled "Be kind to your web-footed friends" all the way to Wyoming, one cherry-headed conure named Ludwig repeatedly singing the opening bars to Beethoven's Fifth, two pied parakeets, and two English parakeets the size of small pigeons, plus an assortment of houseplants.

We would have had an aquarium full of African toads as well, but shortly before we left for Wyoming, we had taken a weekend excursion. Whenever we left overnight, we would leave enough food to see the menagerie through until we returned home the following day. We had done this many times before. We were, therefore, not prepared for what met us. The temperature in the house must have been in the low eighties. The windows were closed and locked against intruders. The curtains had been pulled tight. Everything was secured. Everything but the toads, that is. We had found an occasional toad on the floor before and popped it back into the aquarium without much thought.

This particular evening, we were all tired and hot and eager to drop into soft cushions of sitcom oblivion. I turned the key in the lock. I opened the door. The stench hit me so hard in the face I nearly fell backward off the steps. Foul play was in the air. We had only been gone two days. Could someone have broken into our house and died over the weekend? Could a body smell this badly in just two days?

I entered the house cautiously. I wanted to pull open the drapes in hopes light would change everything. I stepped down and felt something squish and spurt under my foot. I gagged. It was a damn toad. The toads had outgrown their aquarium and had figured out how to push the lid off at will. They had mutinied while we were out. They had taken the house by leaps and bounds. Unfortunately, their freedom was short-lived. They needed water and there was none within their reach. Their skin dried out quickly and soon they were marooned marauders, destined to die in a sea of shag carpet in Kansas, far removed from their African homeland.

Further investigation proved disastrous. All the toads had been sprung.

All had leaped to their deaths. We threw open the windows and cranked up the air conditioning. Stan got a shovel and a trash bag. I got disinfectants and a vacuum. After this, we were all glad to escape the stench of toad and head home to Wyoming for the summer, albeit not without some sense of guilt. Our ruby-rouged little cockatiel did not help to minimize the guilt as he whistled the miles away, "Be kind to your web-footed friends...." I had always thought that referred to ducks, not toads.

Each summer Doug and Sharon were glad to have us back at the clinic. One summer to welcome us back, they invited us out for "hamburgers and hot tubbing." When we arrived, however, Doug was out at the falcon pen. He had the peregrine out. Perched on his forearm, jessied to a leather band on his arm, the bird looked majestic in its steel-gray plumage glinting toward silver. The Rolls Royce of predators.

"Wanna go hunting?" Doug waved to us. "Let's go get some meadowlarks!"

The peregrine in its tooled leather hood sat there like an exotic executioner, its identity hidden to protect its good name. Occasionally a high-pitched cry would indicate it was time to get on with the games ahead.

Doug meticulously examined the bird from hood to toe and weighed it carefully. The bird was light. This was good. It meant it could fly. Doug could release it to hunt with the expectation of its return. If the peregrine weighed heavy, there would be no entertainment this night, for hunting a well-fed bird increased the chance it would not return to the handler. No luxury of anthropomorphizing here. Peregrines are not sentimental. Only a hungry bird will return to a certain meal of pigeon.

We headed north down the dirt road away from curious onlookers. The pomeranian from the neighboring house barked a warning: *Murderers! Thieves!* but no one was around to take heed. Doug decided it would be best to get off the road. It was, after all, decidedly not hunting season. In fact, it was never hunting season on meadowlarks. And if caught hunting, there was more than a mere fine at stake. There was his professional reputation as a veterinarian and at least as importantly, the possibility of having to relinquish his peregrines and hawks. We stepped into the barrow pit and waded through the knee-high grasses. The air was cool; perhaps that was why the hairs on my arms stood up. Doug was scoping the sky. He had removed the hood from the executioner. Adrenaline rushed past us in currents. Not a meadowlark alive could be heard. A land without songbird. Just the eery, high-pitched shriek of the falcon's expectation. The whoosh of reeds against legs, the fierce insistence of mosquito drill. The dusk held on, though low, over the land. Doug released the peregrine and we headed toward the beaver ponds.

The falcon felt the tug of jess give. Instantly, he flapped his wings and rose into the air leaving a momentary scent of warm down in his wake. Then he was free. Higher and higher he rose, circling wider and wider until there on the outer edge of daylight, a small speck of platinum, breast creamy as a cloud, kept a bright black eye targeted dead center on what lay below as it continued in wide gyrations against the dull gray sky. Camouflage complete, he scouted for game. This land seemed never to have heard a bird before. Doug was growing more and more excited, running ahead of us all, head turned to the sky, pointing for us to follow his lead. Earthbound, we trekked onward toward the ponds, crawling through barbed wire fences, sloshing through marshes and cattails, swatting at mosquitoes and dung flies. I felt goosebumps on the back of my neck. We were about to lose the light.

Doug is growing more agitated when there, directly ahead of us, is a beaver pond, and just beyond the cattails sit two mallards. The ducks are a mossy green velvet sitting on the dark mossy water of dusk. *A nice cool swim with a friend, dinner for two at the lake before calling it a duck's day.* But the predator has other plans. Doug is sending signals. The speck at the edge of the sky begins to spiral ever more and more inward, a rippling penny in reverse, as the spirals begin to tighten toward a pinpoint.

Their fear is almost palpable when they notice their plight. Human predators are advancing on their pond. *Fight or flight. Fight or flight.* But just as they notice us approaching, one of them looks up and sees the executioner, hanging there on the troposphere above them like a stain on the sunset.

Terror is not species-specific. The intentional taking of life turns blood cold in any species. Panic makes icy veins boil. Reason is not in the formula. The falcon is circling the pond, so high it is barely visible in this dimming light. The ducks are aflutter, squawking now. Bugs stick in their throats. No need to be silent. Murder is in the air. Caught between a rock and a hard place. Wedged between water and sky. Between human and falcon. All their intuitions tell them to fly. All their intellect tells them to sit planted on that pond.

Fight or flight! Fight or flight! What's a respectable duck to do? You're dead in the water if you don't; you're through if you do. All you wanted was to have a nice quiet dinner for two. You're quite willing to work for mere dung bugs. You don't even expect a dragonfly in every pot. Just a fighting chance. Are there no limits on these weapons of foul destruction?

Sharon and I are tiring of traipsing through the mud in near dusk, tripping in prairie dog holes, swatting at gnats. We are plodding heavily through the muck like weary hippos. Doug and Stan are high on the hunt. The falcon is poised, drawing a bead, hung on the air, holding.

"Run! Wave your arms! Shout and run toward the water!" Doug commands of

Sharon and me. We are reluctant participants. We just want to go home and have dinner. But finally, desperate to be done and goaded by determined hunters, we flail awkwardly toward the water, squawking and thrashing through reeds and cattails. The ducks can hardly believe what they see. They hesitate as if stuck to the surface for one split second before they fly and all hell breaks loose. Intuition has wired them to *fly, fly, fly!*

But there isn't a mallard out there that can fly two hundred kilometers an hour, tearing rips in the path of destruction that is on them *WHOP!* So fast they didn't even see it coming, but they sensed it. Fear prickling their dead duck skin.

The kill was inevitable. They were just sitting ducks. And once the terror of realization was addressed, once the thing finally happened, it was soft. Quiet. Just a muffled *thwump* at pond edge. And then the fall from life. The falcon settling down with graceful gliding dips. It swoops in for the feast.

But there is Doug, Stan behind him, hot and sweating with pleasure, a pigeon to reward the effort. Doug is hooding the executioner who wants only to dive into a good dinner, say, medallions of duck. Sharon and I waddle out of the marshes, glum, our feathers ruffled. We are hungry and just want to eat. We head back through the barbed wire barriers and onto the darkened, dusty road leading us toward the light. The Pomeranian is silent now, having given up on premonitions.

THE HUNT

Selling guns at Gibson's, Pythons were my pride. Jack the price up and tell them, "It's a steal." Take the scope between your eyes for your bandage will be your badge, and they will bring you elk steaks when their wives have gone to church. Smile pretty for the cowboys with the skoal between their teeth. Smile smart for their wives, and don't touch his money, honey.

I admit it. It was just a game to me. Like hopscotch. Just a little hop here, a slight jump there, a bit of a stretch, and there you were. The winner. Or maybe it was more like chess. It did require some finesse. It was a game of wit, I suppose. And flirtation. *Ruger .44 mag., silver with pearl handles, eight-inch barrel, feel that heft?* It was like that. *Honed to a hair trigger.* Raise one eyebrow. *Colt Cobra for your wife? Light as a whisper.* Cock the head coyly. *Detective Special for you--you know, just a little "insurance" inside your boot?* Smile now. *Dan Wesson .357 magnum, three interchangeable barrels, two, four, and six-inch, vent rib, blue or plated. Like having a threesome, isn't it?* You go on this way. *Marlin .22 pump action, sweet little thing to teach your son on.* What's dangerous about nurturance? *Remington 30-06, bolt smooth as warm honey. Winchester .257, sleek, isn't she? Remington shotgun, you can pump that shot home! Want something rougher? Check out this Mauser, 7 millimeter, but only if you think you can handle her kick.* Always with a smile and a well-timed wink. Infallible.

I got bored there, working at Gibson's in the automotive department, selling sparkplugs and oil. There's only so much cleaning one can do around automotive grease. And when the men came in, they came on a mission. Their trucks were not running smoothly. Their fingernails were greasy. They smelled of oil and sweat. Wives were not happy. There were puddles of oil in the driveway. Men were not happy. Weekend football gave way to weekend labor. Selling parts was dirty work with little chance for reward.

Across the aisle, on the other hand, men came for romance. Even the words begged the question: *bait, lure, bobber, tackle, pheasant feather,* and for the more daring, *camouflage, game calls, wild scents--pheromones in a bottle.* But it was the display behind the counter that I fell for. There lay all that was forbidden when I was a child. There, still under lock and key, lay men's toys, all the off-limits guns of my father's closet and more. Only now I had access to the key.

The sporting goods department was run by a man who loved hunting and fishing more than he liked selling and marketing. Norm was a bass fisherman from Kentucky. He was a bird hunter and an antelope, deer, and elk hunter. He stocked the department as if the sporting goods department were his own private toy box. He always had a story or two for anyone who would listen. Fish tales, elk tales. To hear him tell it, he could wrap a fly even you couldn't resist. He could call a moose from its own momma's tit. He never met a fish that wasn't a trophy; he never met an elk without ten points.

In short, the department was falling apart. I found lantern mantles and fishing nets, never displayed or priced, stuffed under shelving. I found packaging, ripped and empty, hanging on pegs. I found fishing weights and lures for Kentucky bass although our streams were filled with trout. I found saltwater reels for our little creeks. I found chaos. Norm had never picked up a feather duster. He ran sales to accommodate his own tackle box. *This department needs a woman's touch*, I thought to myself as I wandered away from Havoline heavy weight and sauntered toward camping gear. It wasn't long until I had every aisle cleaned and polished, every item "faced" on the shelves.

I soon found myself the department manager of sporting goods. I knew nothing of fishing and hunting and camping. I didn't like outdoor activities where I might meet up with bugs, or worse. But I knew how to keep house, and I knew men. Wyoming men. I watched their every movement in the aisles, where they lingered, what they fingered, what their eyes returned to as they walked away. I noticed how often they visited a particular item. I listened to their language. I read the sales catalogs, the bumper sticker politics.

Instead of a manicure set, I carried tiny tools for mounting scopes on hunting rifles, sighting them in on vehicles in the parking lot. Instead of *how is the missus* or *my husband likes this brand too*, I learned to talk the talk of the hunter. I went early one morning at the break of dawn to the shooting range at the edge of town with my bosses, Dick and Tom. They handed me a rifle, a 30.06 bolt, told me to load it. I dropped the sleek brass missiles into the chamber, listened to the cold crack of assurance falling into place.

"Drop to your belly!" Dick commanded. "That'll help you steady the muzzle. You gotta be ready when the big one comes out of the thicket!"

I dropped to the dirt.

"Now snuggle up to the butt real close, baby. Feel its fit in your shoulder."

I snuggled.

"Thatta girl," Tom whispered, his excitement barely contained as though that paper bull's eye pinned to a bale of hay really were a buck.

"Now prop yourself up on your elbow and forearm, and let your left hand sli-i-de down the barrel...slow...slow and gentle...steady...now lean your cheek in...line up the sight...can you see the crosshairs?"

"Ready," I whisper. Tom fidgets.

"Okay...now remember, keep the barrel low. Ready for the kick?" Dick tutors. "When you're ready, and you've got him in your crosshairs, take a deep breath and hold. . . ."

BLAM!

"Ungh," I say, jolting backwards with the kick as my rifle barrel aims for the clouds.

The men are ecstatic. Both of them run for the target, whooping and hollering as though I had shot an eight-point buck. I am dazed. *"Did I wing myself?"* I find myself wondering. My ears are echoing, and my forehead hurts. A trickle of something wet runs down the bridge of my nose. When I touch it, it is sticky and red.

"Good job!" The men praise me even as they examine me. "You hit the target on your very first shot!" Dick takes a handkerchief from his pocket and dabs at my forehead.

"Damn!" Tom exclaims, "I think she's ready for moose!"

I pick myself up and begin to brush myself off. *I did it*, I think with each swipe at the dirt. The pain between my eyes is a little less intense. I lick my upper lip. It tastes of salt and sand, and my teeth are gritty. I stand up, square my shoulders, plant my feet solidly apart, level the barrel once again at my target, knowing now as I do, the game.

I liked the off-season best. January through early August. After that, men start to get itchy. September through December is too easy. Not sporting enough for my tastes. Give me the slow time any day. The time when they don't even know they are hungry. They wander in the front door behind the wives. The wives grab a cart, shopping list and coupons in hand, and head for sewing, or hygiene and beauty, missies and young debs, and finally dog food. The men's eyes are already straying past the check out counters, getting a feel for the lay of the land. They have not spotted me yet, but I am sizing them up across the store.

"Ed!" I say, "See the guy in the red flannel shirt?"

"Yeah, he's a preacher," Ed volunteers. "You better not mess with him. His wife keeps him on the straight and narrow."

"Really?" I say, thinking the gauntlet has just been thrown.

I give him time to find his own way. I am, after all, in the far back of the store, nowhere near anything redeemable. The way I see it is if he wanders that far, he deserves what he finds. What he finds, of course, is the game aisle. And the game today is a *beaut*. A real prize. Hard to find all across the country.

Look at that young girl there behind the counter. What's a sweet young thing like her doing there among the guns? She couldn't possibly know what's what. Maybe I can get a deal on buckshot.

I lean casually against the counter, balancing on my left hip. I can hear him thinking now, so I turn slightly away, and I don't make eye contact. I don't want to scare him off. I wear Chanel. I lean down slowly to unlock the glass counter. I remove the gun. Six-inch Colt Python, silver plate. I run soft flannel over the length of the barrel, hold the Python up to catch the glint of filtered winter light dancing with dust motes all the way to the back of the store.

My God, is that a Python? No, it couldn't be. They're as scarce as a four-point doe. What is the likelihood that this little gal would be the angel of my dreams?

I look up suddenly as though startled by his presence. I smile and say hello. I polish the handle, then get involved in the crevices, frowning slightly. This is too easy.

"That a Python you got there?"

"Why, yes. Yes, it is. You know guns?" I smile and make eye contact. The preacher edges closer to the counter. His neck is flushing. He glances back over his shoulder. The coast is clear.

"Would you like to look at it?" I ask.

"Oh, I shouldn't. I promised my wife no more guns. We barely make it month to month on a preacher's salary." He wants my absolution.

"Well, looking isn't a sin, is it?" I smile.

He reaches out with both arms. He reaches out as though he is giving himself up to Jesus. His forehead is beading with perspiration at his hairline. He has forgotten Prudence, his wife, his promise. He knows all men are sinners and the glory of heaven, after all, rests in redemption.

I place the Python in the palm of his hands. The silver plate steams at his touch. I lean forward on the counter, casual. No sudden moves. I'm aware of everything, the chang-chang-chang of the registers in electronics, the hum of the intercom, on but not in use, and on the local radio station, *Mamas, don't let your babies grow up to be cowboys*, then the sad, sweet story of the cowboy whose wife doesn't understand; I watch as he weighs barrel to grip, see the corners of his mouth soften. It's my cue.

"Nice balance, huh?" I pause, let the ease seep in. "I've been trying to get this piece for months. May not get another this year. This one just arrived."

The preacher is falling in love with the silver, the pearl handles. I've laid the groundwork. Sermon is over.

"Is that your wife over there?"

The preacher is repentant. He offers up the python, places it on the soft red velvet I have laid out on the counter. Says he will come another day, soon. He winks, wipes his brow with his handkerchief, saunters off toward dog food.

It is best not to rush a relationship. Go slow. Let it happen naturally. He liked what he saw; he'll be back.

Next time: recognize him, smile, be happy to see him. But forget about the gun. Ignore the gun. If he asks to look at the gun again, reach for the wrong one. He'll correct you. Then remember. Explain that you forgot which he liked because so many people have looked at guns this week. Mention casually how many men seem to have heard about the Python. Everyone likes it. Confess to him that you think you can sell this gun before the end of the week. Confess to him that lots of men want it badly but also confide that most wives won't allow it. Then tell him about the out-of-town man in the brown felt hat, pheasant feather band, and the custom-made boots. How he usually comes by on Fridays.

You have placed this preacher in purgatory. An angel, yes. A mercenary one. He has heard you loud and clear. *This Beaut is going to be gone by Friday*. He better go home now, get to writing his sermon for Wednesday. It's got to be a winner. That collection plate better runneth over. And maybe a few fine ranchers will come by the rectory with a little something extra if he writes it right, buys them a little wiggle room with their own wives. He's got till Friday.

The last thing I do Wednesday before closing is prepare the ad copy for Friday morning. I prepare an ad for .357 magnum shells. I write in small print, *"Every day low price,"* and in larger print, I write *"no more than six boxes per customer"* on bright red paper and hang it on the shelf. It always works. People stock up on such ads. Then I make a real ad for leather holsters and belts, ten percent off will do it. I am prepared.

Friday morning I head straight for the gun closet. I distribute the handguns in the glass counter, polish the glass. All but one, that is. I leave the Python for last, take it from its box, shine it up inside and out. I spin the cylinder. It purrs back like a kitten. I smile at the thought. Who would think this thing has bite? I lock the Python up.

At ten o'clock sharp the front doors open. A few people saunter in. One heads toward the film counter. One looks dressed for an interview. Another, greasy, heads toward spark plugs. A woman and two little kids head into the milk aisle. The children beg for animal crackers until the mother gives in.

They eat a few as they wander down the aisle. Soon, the mother is engrossed in the percentage of fat in hamburger and the children escape to play in the toy aisle. It's a typical Friday.

It's ten thirty when the preacher walks in. He's not with his wife. He's not even dressed in preacher's clothes. He's in Levis, a plaid western shirt, and boots. He is Everyman, but he looks like another hefty commission to me. A mid-quarter raise when the district manager comes through town. An expense-paid trip to Dallas to buy more guns. Bragging rights with the guys who work for me. One more gold star glued to the side of the cash register, a star for every gun I've sold.

I busy myself with a feather duster going over the rack of long guns. I keep my back to him. Don't scare him off. Let him make the approach. Let him play *alpha*. I hear the boots on polished linoleum about half an aisle away. He pauses. I estimate he's made it as far as the *SALE!* sign in the holster aisle. I spray myself with just a touch of Chanel No. 22 from the atomizer I keep under the counter.

"Morning, ma'am," I hear his southern drawl as I turn toward him.

"Good morning, Reverend. What can I do for you?" I ask innocently. He is already bent over the glass counter, staring in.

"Oh, I shouldn't even be back here," he confesses. "My wife would have a fit."

"Well, Reverend," I wink, "who is going to tell her?" I am unlocking the gun counter. I slide the door open. My fingertips touch the pearl handle. I look up at him, smile, and say, "Would you like to hold it?" I see him hesitate. He seems a little flighty, so I add, "It might not be here tomorrow, you know. In fact, I bet it's gone by the end of the day."

The man didn't run. He didn't turn his back and head straight out the door he came in. It was as though his feet were caught in some hunter's trap and he couldn't even squirm himself free. He stood there, dead in my sights, as I handed him the Python. Again he felt its balance, twirled the cylinder, polished the pearl. He laid it quickly down on the red velvet bed on the counter and fished for his wallet.

Whap!

I got him, I thought. His Mastercard hit the glass with a smack. I told myself to calm down, do it right. His eyes were wild. I handed him a pen and pushed the papers in front of him. I watched him check "no" in every box without taking the time to read. He signed the paperwork and dated it. It was over before he even knew what hit him. We were done.

This was Wyoming. There was no waiting period. Just a driver's license I.D. and a signature on a piece of paper. I locked up the gun counter and added another gold star under my name on the side of the register, my version of another "notch on my gun." Everything else I would do for the day would be gravy. Pure profit.

The preacher was only one of many. There was my next door neighbor, a widow with three small children to support, who came to me two weeks before her birthday with a special request: *Please don't sell my fiancé another rifle for my birthday. I really need a washing machine.* Her words rang clearly in my ear as I handed the man his latest acquisition. She couldn't appear ungrateful on her birthday. But I too had a family to feed, bills to pay, I reminded myself when necessary.

That is the philosophy I adopted after the heist. I was not the dishonest one. I was not the thief. I had the paperwork to prove it. There was nothing illegal about selling guns. Then one late winter day, on my one day off, the phone rang around six thirty in the morning. *Break in? Guns gone?* I had to shake my head to convince myself I was not dreaming. But Dick's voice rose in excitement on the other end of the line. No time to shower. Just get dressed. The police were waiting. Only I knew the inventory well enough at a glance to tell what was missing, how many, which kind. Only I could tell what was out of place, rearranged. *Hurry. Lives could be at stake.*

Lives could be at stake. I was waking up. Who would do this? Who would break in and take the guns *without paperwork?* I had never imagined anyone would do anything bad with a gun I sold. Even the time the cowboy came up to me as I stood alone at the counter, pointed a .44 magnum at me and said, "Give me all your money," it never occurred to me that he might actually mean it. I just smiled and made a smart remark back to him as I reached out and pushed the barrel aside. Cowboys like women with *chutzbah.* Or the time the woman pulled the .38 snub nose detective special out of her purse, and pointing it directly at me, said, "Do you know what kind of bullets this takes?" A good hunter never blinks.

I sold where it was appropriate when I could. I sold to the ranchers and the sportsmen in town. I didn't to the kid whose mind was so fried that he once showed up in cowboy boots, a western shirt, and boxer shorts, unaware he had forgotten anything. And I didn't to the felon from my hometown, recently out of prison, even though he assured me he wouldn't tell.

So I mounted scopes on rifles for hunting season. I sold shells and holsters and camping equipment for frosty nights in a tent. And I challenged myself, depending on the season, to sell a gun a day or in February, one a week. I trained the men to come to me, feeding them little crumbs of fantasy here, a tidbit of hope there. I worked with them all year long, so when the time came, they were mine for the picking, so-to-speak.

I was unprepared, however, that Monday morning when the front doors unlocked and the preacher and his wife walked in. He was wearing his collar. She was leading and did not stop in grocery. He followed close behind. They walked straight to the back of the store, but instead of coming to my counter, she led him right past the lures and bait and straight to the manager's office. The preacher glanced sheepishly in my direction but kept his head low.

They were gone for about thirty minutes before I heard my name over the intercom, *Anita, come to the manager's office, please.* Dick always came to our counter if he had something to say to us. We never got called to his inner sanctuary. What could this mean? I had done the paperwork by the book when I sold the preacher the gun.

I opened the door to the office. The preacher and his wife were gone. There sat Dick at his desk, the box open before him. He stared glumly at the shiny pistol, the Colt Python, one of the most coveted weapons in the country. He looked up at me, a helpless, defeated look on his face and shoved the box in my direction.

"Take it," he said. "Clean it up and put it back in the case. Destroy the paperwork. It's not been shot. You can sell it as new."

The story began to unfold. The family was barely making it on food stamps and welfare. She grew a garden and canned. He hunted and they packaged the game. It got them through. But there was no insurance and the little one had asthma. She had an ulcer. And the preacher could preach but not much else. She had saved everything she could during the summer by selling her produce. She had picked wild berries that grew in the hills to make jellies to sell. She took from the hand-me-downs and throw-aways at the parish to provide for her family. She pieced quilts. She and the children maintained the little church and grounds for a small stipend. She kept all she earned carefully under her own surveillance, a necessity she had learned through experience.

The Mastercard was only for emergency asthma attacks. Ruptured ulcers. Things that couldn't wait for pay day. Not for Pythons. Not for pearl handles and silver plating. Not for special etching. Not for dreams. Not for wild goose hunts. Not for a smile and the scent of Chanel 22. The Mastercard was not the path to the pearly gates. Repentance and humility were the way. Dick had agreed to cancel the charge and take back the gun. The man was, after all, a man of God.

I felt badly for marking the preacher. I knew all along his wife would be the one to pay the consequences. And seeing her walk through the front door that way, dowdy and resolute, the preacher reduced to a whimpering penitent, she was oddly dignified in her shame. So I took back the gun, examined it closely, cleaned and polished all fingerprints from it, and placed it carefully back in the glass counter in the very spot it had occupied four days earlier. Equilibrium had been restored. The problem was in the stars. They weren't so easy to take back. I sprayed them with cleanser and scrubbed at the cash register, but even after I carefully peeled away the gold stars, still you could see, indelibly etched in the constellations there, my undeniable love of the hunt.

FAIR GAME

In mid-January, 1991, I was middle-aged, single, and filled with optimism. Outside, the January air prickled my skin. It stung my ears and burned inside my nostrils. It reminded me of what it meant to be alive. Inside, I sipped champagne and watched the news with the new man in my life.

All the news commentators were vying for air, caught up in the drone of scuds. All their questions were the same. *How many casualties? What kind of fire power? Where is Sad-dam?* It was the Desert Storm. The wires buzzed, electrified with the word, *war. . . war. . . war. . . .*

I put my feet up, and curled like a cat on the couch, I watched as the commentator described what the camera lens caught—"little arms and hands wriggling up out of the sand"—as our great American bulldozers swept up the desert.

Clean up. Clean up. And if it can't be scoured clean, cover it over. What is it in our affluent American backgrounds that makes us obsessive in our need for efficiency, our need to sweep up, put everything in its place?

Cover is everything and scuttle along is all most of us do. Pests may be all we are. And somehow, the cold dreariness beyond the television screen seemed then, and now, reason enough to huddle closer together, to scramble for safety in our own way in order not to be obliterated in the vacuum of our American mores.

How is it that, as the third of three daughters, born to a father who never went to war and a mother who pursued her own career, I learned quickly the games of predation? In my red felt cowgirl hat, I practiced twirling my silver cap guns and shooting at imaginary enemies. Nothing delighted me more than to track Terry, the neighbor nearest my age, through the pasture and into the orchard, keeping low and still. I knew instinctively that silence was my guardian. We would stalk each other monotonously morning after morning.

Crab apple season was a favorite of ours. It ranked right up there with a good, wet snowfall. Crab apples were our grenades. They were best for this while the crabs were still hard. As the crabs ripened, they became missiles of deadly gases, and passing vehicles were not Old Man Marcus on his way to the pool hall or the neighbor lady volunteering at the thrift shop. The bright yellow Mustang Mach-III that Terry's older brother Bud raced looked like an enemy tank to us. The scent of souring crab apples was, in our imagination, the scent of deadly gases propelled through the air at our *non-stationary targets*. We had already learned by then not to call them *people*. We knew we were not to shoot at people, but we also understood that people called by any other name were fair game. It was not until years later that I understood why we refer to *soft targets* and *collateral damage* when what we really mean is "people."

In the winter we waited like children for a good snowfall, wet, heavy and deep. At the break of day, we all went into action. The whole neighborhood, kindergarteners to early teens, was recruited. We rolled the snow into bigger and bigger snow boulders, tamping it down as we moved forward, leaving trails that turned into foxholes and ravines. The younger recruits would line up the huge balls to form fortress walls. The older recruits would hoist snowball after snowball upward, shaping the walls as our predecessors had done before us. We would bring pitchers of water to dab on the walls, fortifying them with ice. Our buttresses would last for weeks. We stockpiled snowballs. Sometimes it was Baker kids against Cortez kids. Sometimes it was older kids versus younger ones. Sometimes it was male versus female. The wars came and went. We learned the strategies of survival, the perils of loss, the adrenaline rush of victory. We plotted raids on each others' forts, stealing ammunition and learning along the way that it was even more fun if we left evidence to show who had conducted this act of brave misconduct. We learned the psychology of war. The more outrageous our behavior, the greater the shame in defeat, the higher the high of victory. It was here I first experienced penis envy. I learned that boys could desecrate a snow fort in ways that I could not.

From travels with my father in the badlands, I had learned that people had had to scavenge for food when food was scarce. I was gifted with a plentiful imagination, so I spent one summer exploring our land and figuring out what Terry and I could live on, were another war to rear its ugly head in the neighborhood. I knew where and how to find angle worms, and I could collect them and feed them on coffee grounds, but I had no intention of eating the things. Better to give them to my father and let him catch trout which I would then eat, thereby consuming the worm, I reasoned.

I turned my attention to grasshoppers. They were more interesting because of their ability to hop, fly, and produce a rattling sound much like a rattlesnake. They also fought back by spitting a nasty brown substance we deemed poisonous tobacco. I caught them by the jarsful. I had an old butter knife and a fork, stolen from my mother's kitchen drawer. These were my instruments of triage. I would retrieve a grasshopper from the jar, pull off his legs and wings to *de-mobilize* him. Then I proceeded to study him, sometimes slicing through his abdomen to study him from the inside out, sometimes decapitating him. An old rolling pin would flatten him right out and a hammer would pulverize him.

I was considering all the ways to turn grasshopper into C-rations when my father the CIA happened upon my "kitchen *mess.*" He, never having been to war, misinterpreted my intentions as unnecessary torture and took away my equipment. About this time I noticed the lilacs in full bloom, saw the bees buzzing among them and decided to explore the culinary possibilities of flowers. Fortunately, our yard was filled with nasturtiums, pansies, and dandelions, all edible when added to a salad.

In July we turned our attentions to paratrooper training. We lived on the Heights, the area up on the bluffs above town, the river running far below. The bluffs were forbidden to me, and though there was a narrow dirt path that wound the length of the bluff all the way to the Bighorn River bridge, my mother had implanted plenty of stories in me over the years to reinforce the expectation that I never, ever go near that path. We kids heard about the old man who wandered too near the edge after an evening at the bars in town and slipped over and was not found until morning, a crumpled up mess of mud and stale beer found by boys on a carp hunt. "*Even a drunken stupor could not save him,*" my mother made clear. And there was the story of the teenage boy who took the turns to his girlfriend's house too fast and they both ended up at the bottom of the river. "*Hormones are a fast-track to tragedy,*" Mother said, her eyebrow raised. I didn't know what hormones were, but I knew I didn't want anything to do with them.

Instead, Terry and I spent our time planning escapes from our enemies. One of the best was Terry's idea. By July, the wild cucumber vines were thickly knotted all up and down the bluff. We expected one day to be chased to the edge of the bluff by our mortal enemies, our older siblings. It would be life or death, Terry said, to know how to survive when we went over the edge. "*Come on,*" he coaxed, "*are you game?*"

He taught me how to sit and slide close to the precipice, dangling my feet as I grabbed hold of the clots of vine, netted my arms with the scratchy tendrils, the prickly cucumbers my lifeline. The older kids, he assured me weighed too much to try this, so we would be safe. I dug my toes into the green ropes, closed my eyes, and trusted in Terry's wisdom. I let go of the bluff. I was transported into thin air, no longer connected to the world below.

This must be what it is like, I thought, to die. Why do people fight it so hard?

The vine reached its limits and slammed me back against the bluff. I felt something pop in my elbow and a searing pain followed. My face was scratched and I lost my grip. The river waited below. I felt panic. I heard my mother's words, *hormones are a fast-track to tragedy*. Were hormones like poison ivy?

Terry was back on the path, lying on his belly in the soft dirt, his hands extended toward me as far as he could reach. His face was contorted with something like fear or determination as he reached down over the edge and pulled me toward him. My knees were bloody from trying to climb to safety. As I pulled myself back onto the path, I was too relieved to be mad at Terry for instigating the game. I was more worried about hiding our game from an anxious mother at home.

The summer of 1968, I was seventeen. The war in Viet Nam was in full swing. The television news was obsessed with it. People could recite body counts like baseball scores. Even so, the war seemed far removed from me in north central Wyoming. Viet Nam meant a plethora of pen pals. It was the patriotic thing for a young teenage girl to do. It was the equivalent of Rosie the Riveter.

Terry joined the Marines and away he went. We were going to visit my sister Lisa who was in the Women's Army Corps at Fort Devens, Massachusetts. She was the only female member of the Menehune Platoon. The Menehune Platoon consisted of a platoon of guys of Asian descent, many of them from Hawaii. My new brother-in-law who was known as "Kane" (short for Kaneshiro) was a sort of Japanese combination of Elvis Presley and Don Ho, and the platoon was popular for their luaus on the nearby beaches on their nights off. They played Hawaiian tunes and strummed ukeleles. They shed their khakis for loin cloths and danced the hula while some of the more talented guys performed Tahitian torch dances. They roasted whole pig on a spit and everyone dipped their fingers in the communal pot of poi. Mai tais and leis were the party signatures, and drunken colonels' wives were discreetly not recognized the next day.

On duty days they ran a mock POW camp in the Massachusetts forest. They were the Viet Cong. They wore black pajamas and straw hats taken straight from the rice paddies of Viet Nam. They carried AK-47s and grenades. It was part of the training for soldiers heading to combat. Soldiers would go through classes and training maneuvers to prepare for the guerilla warfare of the Southeast Asian jungle. They were introduced to the strategic moves of the jungle: *Take two steps forward, one step backward. Do not step off to the side of the path. You will not be given a free pass.* This was serious play. The trip wires buried in vines just off the pathway, stumbled upon, could impale a soldier with stakes the length of his whole body. Camouflaged drop holes, just big enough for a man, could become a lonely grave. *Follow the instructions,* was the mantra, *or you will become fair game.*

Soldiers sent for survival training before being shipped to Viet Nam would be set loose in the Massachusetts jungle of Fort Devens just about dusk. This was the last exercise before graduation. They had orders to find a village harboring the Viet Cong, capture the village and locate the Viet Cong in it, then wait for further instructions.

One night while visiting my sister, we were given permission to join the games and spend the night in the jungle. We would only be allowed to observe, not actively participate. We dressed in black since we would be with the Viet Cong. A little before dusk we positioned ourselves on a hill in the woods above one of the Vietnamese villages. The Menehunes told us stories of how they had been discriminated against as Asians on base during the day and how they had their revenge at the camps after dark. The sun was setting. We had seen the intercom speakers camouflaged in the trees around the village as we climbed to our position, but no speakers were near where we sat quietly waiting for what, we did not know. Shortly after dark we heard voices in the distance. We grew silent and watchful. I felt the adrenaline beginning to surge through me.

"Back up a little higher on the hill," my brother-in-law whispered to us.

We could see the soldiers now approaching the village. They were excited. They had not expected to come upon the village so early in the evening. If they captured it quickly and routed out the "V.C.," they could be home in their beds by midnight. Their platoon would get the special commendations at the graduation ceremony tomorrow.

They quietly worked their way in close to the village, branching out to surround its circumference. They could see the village from all angles now, but there were no people left in the village. They must have feared the G.I.s approach and abandoned the place earlier in the day. The G.I.s sent in some scouts. The scouts approached cautiously. There was no resistance. No one in sight. They approached the huts and one by one pushed open the doors and peered inside. No one. The village was vacant. Not even a dog sniffed around. Just abandoned huts and something that looked like old cornshucks tied together scattered here and there. The scouts motioned the "all clear" sign and the whole platoon began to advance on the village.

Once in the village, they began to relax a bit. They had taken the village. That was their orders. Mission accomplished. Bed by midnight. They established guards around the periphery and everyone settled in to open their C-rations. As they ate, they began to feel jubilant. Graduation was tomorrow and then they were off to fight the good battle, to save the world from communism and gooks. Camaraderie had been established. They told jokes about what the women over there could teach the G.I.s' wives. They shared stories about the weed available. *If Cong gooks are as dumb as the gooks in this camp, war is going to be a goddamn cakewalk.*

The atmosphere was celebratory. Then suddenly, out of nowhere it seemed, a woman's voice, soft and seductive: "Hello, G.I." The camp grew silent except for the hurried shuffling as men put down their C-rations and reached for their weapons.

"Does your mama know where you are tonight, G.I.?" the sexy voice whispered through the trees. There was some shuffling down below.

"Here's something for your mama!" a G.I. hollered back at the hill.

"Watch out for fire," my brother-in-law whispered. By now, we were no longer in a Massachusetts forest and grenades and weapons were not firing blanks. G.I.s had become the enemy. We were no longer curious bystanders. The cloak of night had transformed the land. We were Viet Cong and these intruders wanted us dead.

The grenade sailed through the darkness, the tell-tale whistle off to our east marking it as harmless. No one responded. We met it with silence. The soldiers didn't know what to do. They had wanted something. A death scream. Gunfire. Something they could react to. No one had taught them how to respond to silence. We could hear them discussing their situation. There was disagreement in the camp and the soldier in charge seemed unsure of his next move. We sat on the hillside, our patience weighing heavily upon us. The soldiers took a few pot shots into the woods and drew no response. The G.I.s returned to their C-rations but silently now. The night air was heavy and humid.

"Did you say your prayers tonight, G.I.?" My sister's airy whisper seemed to dance through the trees, picked up on a breeze.

The soldiers had had enough. They jumped to their feet, commands rang out below. Bullets and grenades littered the air. They were firing in all directions. The soldiers had formed a ring around the village and facing out, were firing into the trees. We backed up the hill while the Menehunes drew fire away from us by shooting a bullet here or there or by throwing a stick into the trees opposite us.

The soldiers continued to stare out into the darkness. No one noticed that the shocks of corn had changed position inside the village. Slowly the Viet Cong, deftly hidden inside the shocks, had been moving in on the G.I.s.

until the G.I.s found themselves surrounded. The Menehunes gave a yell and all flooded the village with black pajamas, AK-47s waving in their hands, as they shouted commands in a language the G.I.s could not comprehend.

In no time at all, the soldiers were rounded up, bound, and marched single file through the New England woods. Midnight came and went. They arrived at a hut on the outskirts of a fenced camp. The camp had barbed wire fencing around it.

One of the Menehunes recognized the first lieutenant who had asked my sister earlier in the week why a pretty thing like her was sleeping with a *slant-eye*. The Menehune told the lieutenant as he approached the camp to shout over and over again, "Lisa's fat and ugly! Lisa's fat and ugly!"

"Drop to the ground!" my brother-in-law commanded of the G.I. Kane's eyes fell on the first lieutenant and he recognized the man who had made the offensive remark to his wife earlier in the week at the PX. "Drop!" he demanded again when the lieutenant did not oblige quickly enough, and with a shove, Kane assisted the lieutenant to the ground.

"I want to see you doing push ups and I want to hear you singing out loud and clear, 'One for Lisa, two for Lisa' until I tell you to quit, you sorry bastard!" Even my parents, watching from the sidelines, seemed transformed by hatred.

Inside the hut, interrogations were being conducted. G.I.s were being connected with a line straight through to Ho Chi Minh. Their fingertips were wired. When they did not provide the answer the Menehunes in charge were looking for, they received a small electrical charge. It did not seem to bother most of them at first, the charge was so minute. But question after question was fired at them, each time in a more hostile voice, each time with a promise of higher voltage until the volley of questions and promised shocks began to alter their consciousness. In a matter of minutes, even young officers were begging for mercy. But the more one begged, the more one got.

After leaving the interrogation hut, prisoners of war were dispersed throughout the camp for their own designer night of games. Some were left in huts alone to wait the night away to see how they adjusted to the long unknown. Others were worn down physically as well as psychologically. I watched Kane interrogate a soldier fatigued with hours of calisthenics. He would take a long drag on a cigarette, then ask the soldier a question. If the soldier refused to give the answer Kane sought, he would blow smoke in the G.I.'s face, hold the cigarette close to the soldier's eyes, and touch his eyelid with the tip of an ice cube concealed in the palm of his hand. I watched as the soldier screamed as though his eyes were being burned right out of their sockets.

The most resistant soldiers were tied to a pole and left, their arms and legs bound in place, muscles stretched to their limits of endurance. Their only escape came through sobs, divulgence, and total humiliation. One man soiled himself the night I stood watching. They left the camp the next morning wearing their humiliation, not yet aware they would carry it as their shield into combat the very next week half a world away.

The strongest soldiers were the ones who never stopped looking for a means of escape. They wore a mask of compliance while waiting, watching, listening. Such soldiers might be given an opportunity to overhear two Menehunes talking Pidgin English. They might hear scraps of conversation, something about an escape route if the *Charlie* were overcome. Something about a tunnel under the floor under the cot in an interrogation hut. Such soldiers might try a friendly gesture toward the enemy or just be grateful for a moment of isolation. As the night wears on, the V.C. might grow complacent, might even nod off a bit outside the hut. Across the camp there might be a distraction as some poor sucker draws the attention of the camp. *This is it, now or never*, a soldier might conclude as he felt under the cot with his bound hands. There is a spot like a line. Bolstered now by this discovery, he wriggles his wrists until the rope loosens. He slips out of the binding and with a glance toward the door, he is quickly under the cot, forgotten in shadow. He traces the line in the wood, finds a knothole, and lifts toward him. Still no sound outside the hut. What sorry bastard is providing his cover, he wonders. He finds the hole, just big enough to edge into. He goes head first and pulls himself into the earth. It is cold and damp and smells of rot and dead fish but it is definitely a tunnel. He can't stop to consider anything now. His actions have made his choices. He closes his eyes and tells himself not to panic. This hole leads somewhere. Cobwebs brush his face. His hand reaches forward and touches something moist and alive, he thinks. *Don't think*, he tells himself, *just move forward*. It is hard to breathe. He can't afford to panic now. *Remember when we used to play Sardines as a kid, how one kid would hide and then everyone would hunt for the hiding place, joining with the hidden until the last hunter uncovered the secret place. This is just a game of hide and seek*, he might tell himself, inching along in the dark.

And when finally he sees some light at the end of the tunnel, he is afraid to hope it's real. But he can't afford not to believe either, so he keeps edging himself forward, and then there it is, light. And air. Suddenly he doesn't remember the earlier lessons of the evening. Dusk seems ions ago. He has forgotten that silence can be camouflage too, and when he pops his head up out of the ground and into the light, he opens his eyes to a blur of black movement. He has spent the night crawling through rotten undergrowth only to come up for air into the light of the camp, AK-47s aimed at his head.

Stay calm, he tells himself. *They can't break you if you refuse to be broken. War requires a complicit agreement. Round and round the mulberry bush, the fox chases the weasel. . . . Stay calm, don't let your fear show. Cover up. Round and round. . . .*

The sun is peeking over the eastern horizon. Daylight has returned the landscape to Massachusetts. Off to the west, I can see the interstate traffic carrying the commuters to work. All the soldiers are wearing uniforms of the United States Army. I am going shopping for a new swimsuit later today. I am seventeen and on vacation in New England and this is Summer Camp, U.S.A.

A MATTER OF PERSPECTIVE

The thing about insanity is that it looks like sanity if you look it straight in the eye. It's only if you look slightly askance that you can get a glimpse of it.

The day Stan graduated from veterinary school was a momentous occasion in our family. All of our families came for the ceremony. I got my first new dress in almost a year, picked from Walmart earlier in the week. Jason got new pants, shirt, and shoes that weren't scuffed. Stan got a new tie.

The ceremony was less than memorable. I am sure there were speeches, organ music, and cheers from the audience. It was all superfluous. What was uppermost in our minds was what we had come through and especially, where we were heading. This great achievement that we had held up before us for so long had finally been attained. We had held it out there as the motivator when we were short on groceries. When we were short on tuition. When we were short on nerves. It was the thing that got us through. *Graduation.* Anything that went wrong in our lives got dismissed or explained away as we kept our eyes focused dead straight ahead on our future. The Future was what made sense now. *Our* future had finally arrived.

Unlike most of the graduates, we did not have to hunt for jobs. We had known from the beginning that we had a job waiting for us in Wyoming after graduation. Stan had, in fact, been "practicing" behind the scenes for a couple summers already. Doug and Sharon were looking forward to our permanent return so that Doug would have more time to pursue his first love—falconry. Stan was happy too because he would have ample opportunity to get a lot of experience quickly.

Once the celebrations were over, we quickly packed up our possessions and headed for the western horizon. Sharon had found a house we could "sit." The owner was a never-married French professor who was going on an anthropological dig site in Lebanon for the summer. She was an anthropologist by training, a French speaker by birth, and an eccentric by nature. She had grown up in Belgium. She loved animals (and therefore, veterinarians) and dead cultures more than people. The house was large and airy and decorated with authentic, old Persian rugs and musty Spanish antiques. Nieman Marcus catalogs littered the shelves. We could bring our menagerie of one cat and seven birds with us. We would not have to pay rent. All we would have to do was look after her two geriatric dogs, Monsieur and Madame Rampeau, and a cat, Mademoiselle Katnippe, and thirty-two lovebirds, all with names, which lived in a long flight cage perched the length of the kitchen cabinet. Our adventure was about to begin.

The first thing we did was move the birds into a room of their own. The second thing I did was scrub the kitchen for two days straight, trying to make the counters usable. Although I scraped, scrubbed, and cloroxed ad nauseum, we found feather fragments floating in our tea for the three months we lived there.

By the end of the summer, I had found the perfect little starter house. It was across the park from the professor's large home and had a wonderful view of the mountains to the east. We moved the lovebirds back to the kitchen counter and began moving into our very own first house. Stan was now a doctor, I was the doctor's wife, and we had a son, a cat, and seven birds. The only thing we lacked now to be legitimate was a dog. A veterinarian without animals is not a veterinarian to be trusted.

I answered an ad in the local paper: *Beagles for sale*. I went to check out the beagles. I drove to a fashionable neighborhood and found the address. The house was two stories with a big, lichen-covered chimney on one end and a huge veranda curled around two sides of the house. The place seemed deserted but I stepped to the door and rang the bell. The air burst into a frenzy of loud bays and barks. A woman came to the door.

"Come on in," she said as she bent over to scoop up three beagle pups in one fell swoop, "but be careful where you step. You might step on a beagle— or worse!" She laughed at her own joke.

I stepped inside and quickly learned that it was no joke. There were seven puppies and two adult beagles all running around the room. There were squeak toys and well-used chew bones littering the parquet floor. There were dishes of dog chow in the kitchen and dishes of water, dabs and dribbles sprinkling the floor. The place smelled of damp dog food and damp carpet. It made lovebirds on the kitchen counter seem sane.

Beagles were everywhere, tumbling over each other, bouncing up and down at my ankles. One was growling loudly and tugging at an old sock a boy was swinging back and forth. They were pudgy, cute little pups. The woman began giving me their bloodlines. They were from a long line of champion show dogs. One little guy began to bay as if on cue.

"Wouldn't he be something on a fox hunt?" the woman suggested. "Check them all out. They are all for sale, three hundred dollars a piece, except for that little girl over there. She is due for the long sleep at the vet's office first chance I can get away."

"The long sleep?" I asked. I had no idea what she meant.

"She's a reject. See that kink in her tail? She looks like a little piglet, doesn't she?" the woman giggled.

"Oh, I think she is adorable!" I replied. "I want her!"

"Oh, that's not possible," the woman explained. "She has bad genes. She can't be shown, and I can't have her hurting my bloodline. I've got to get rid of her."

Her bloodline, I thought; *whose* bloodline? I wanted the little beagle more than ever when I realized she was about to die for a kink in her perky little tail.

"Oh, please let me take her," I begged. "My husband is a veterinarian and I promise to have her spayed. I just want her for a companion."

The woman began to soften. Eventually we came to terms: No papers. The beagle would be spayed as early as possible, and I would tell no one where I had purchased the dog. The hidden secrets of her champions would be secure. I paid the woman twenty-five dollars, *cash only*, snapped the pup up, and was out the door with my bargain basement beagle before she could change her mind.

I rushed home to pick up Jason, then on to the clinic to surprise Stan with our new family member. It was love at first sight for all of us. Stan examined her. She had a most definite crook in her tail which only added to her bubbly personality. She was a beautiful tri-color destined to be small in frame. Her face was friendly and her kinky little tail never seemed to stop waggling. I named her Tulip Marie. It was only over the years that we learned she also had a soft pallet and hip dysplasia, both of which bothered her more as she aged.

We met most of the town through the veterinary clinic. I worked there off and on just to help out and also to be a part of things. I was not as naturally at ease with strangers' animals as Stan and most everyone else at the clinic. That, of course, made me the preferred target of many a clinic prank.

The day Mrs. Fredericks came in with her cat, the entire staff had noted her name in the appointment log and carefully arranged to be very busy at the time of her arrival. Everyone but me, that is. I didn't know anything except that an established client was bringing her cat in to be checked for a skin condition. Skin conditions were fairly uncommon since Wyoming did not have fleas. It was usually just dry skin or perhaps, ringworm. This was a housecat, so ringworm was less likely.

I'm pretty good, I thought to myself. *I've already diagnosed this cat and it's not even in the door yet!* Mrs. Fredericks opened the door and approached the counter.

"Good morning!" I said cheerily, wanting word to spread quickly that the new vet's wife was friendly.

Mrs. Fredericks did not answer. Her cat Sweetums was stuffed precariously under one arm. She rummaged through her purse for a notepad and two pens, one red, one black. I waited. Sweetums squirmed. Mrs. Fredericks put the notepad down on the counter and began to draw two red circles. She laid down the red pen and picked up the black pen. She drew four lines, bent in the middle, on each side of both circles. She laid down the black pen and picked up the red pen. Sweetums was beginning to make a low growling sound under her armpit. Mrs. Fredericks made smaller round circles in solid red all over the inside of the large circle. She picked up the black pen and made a little dot in the center of each reddened circle.

I stood there. Was this a joke? I didn't know what to say. Mrs. Fredericks wrote at the top of the page in large, all capital letters: WHAT ARE THESE? She shoved the paper toward me.

I looked at the paper. I looked at her and smiled, realizing finally this *is* a joke!

"I haven't the slightest idea," I replied. "Are they itsy bitsy spiders?" I immediately felt foolish.

Mrs. Fredericks planted the angry cat on the countertop and leaned heavily over him to anchor him to the counter. She wrote: THEY ARE SPIDERS? WHAT KIND AND HOW DO I GET RID OF THEM?

I was getting my education as a veterinarian's wife. I learned that day that *anything* you say can be taken as diagnosis.

"Well, no," I explained, "I don't really know what they are. I thought you were going to tell me."

"IF I KNEW WHAT THEY WERE, I WOULDN'T HAVE TO PAY A VETERINARIAN TO TELL ME, WOULD I?" she wrote back, making sense finally.

"Uh, no, that's true," I admitted. "Let me see if I can find the doctor for you." As I came around the corner, the entire clinic staff was there, some with their hands planted firmly across their mouths, some almost doubled over, all laughing unceremoniously at my initiation to Mrs. Fredericks.

I was relieved when, at long last, Doug agreed to see Mrs. Fredericks and her cat. He asked me, however, to come into the room to help hold the cat. I reluctantly followed him into the exam room. As Mrs. Fredericks placed the cat on the cold, stainless steel table, the cat lost all patience. Its black hair stood on end, it hissed, it growled, and it struck out with all claws bared. Mrs. Fredericks's forearms were the unlucky recipients.

The cat jumped from the table, sprang off her arms, and landed on the clinic curtains, swinging for its life, trailing the unmistakable scent of cat urine behind it.

Mrs. Fredericks began to omit an odd keening sound. I looked at her and saw her arms. The scratches were an irritated red in the midst of white splotches up and down her arms. She almost looked tie-dyed. Later, once Doug had captured and contained Sweetums, given Mrs. Fredericks a moisturizing shampoo to cleanse the urine from the demon, and sent them on their way, the whole clinic began to tell me her story. She was a diagnosed schizophrenic. She had taught her cat to be also. She imagined little bugs on her skin which she said came from the cat, so she bathed herself in bleach against her physician's warnings. Every now and then it got so bad that she had to be hospitalized for a while and that is when Sweetums would come to stay with us. Sadly, they said, it was always about the time that Sweetums started to behave like a normal housecat that Mrs. Fredericks would come home and the whole cycle would begin again.

Lesson two in being a veterinarian's wife: Crazy people may be pet owners. I learned that crazy people sometimes have crazy pets. Upon reflection I realized that crazy people are people too. They deserve compassion. Urinating flying cats, on the other hand—well, that's a more difficult consideration.

What was it about a veterinary hospital that brought people's quirks out into the light of day? I began to imagine sanity as a kind of kaleidoscope and all the jagged variations of design and color were all the slight deviations that could be derived from what we think of as sanity. If the things that I considered a little odd seemed perfectly normal to someone else, was I the odd one out or were they? Who knew?

When the well-dressed woman brought in the Vizla, she was somewhat high-strung but polite. The dog was about two years old, she said, and absolutely devoted to her husband. They went everywhere together. The dog even slept at the foot of the bed on her husband's side. Now her husband, a local policeman, had been sent to a special training school for twelve weeks, and the dog had done nothing but whimper and refuse to eat since he left. To make matters worse, she needed to leave immediately to care for her terminally ill mother who lived in Arizona in a pet-free complex. The Vizla was so neurotic that she was sure it could not adjust to a new owner. The only humane thing to do, she had reasoned, was to euthanize it. Put it out of its pain. She was distraught but certain she was doing what had to be done.

It was sad but perfectly rational. She needed to make her mother's illness a priority over the loss of the dog.

We watched her come to terms with the difficult circumstances. The dog was young and beautiful, but it was neurotic. It couldn't adjust to living with anyone else. It wouldn't make a good pet for anyone. We all understood that euthanasia was the right thing to do.

The woman was impressive in her handling of the situation. She did not cry. She was stoic. Having made the decision, she quickly handed the leash to one of the assistants who led the dog to the back. She signed the euthanasia form without hesitation. This was a woman of resolution followed by action. I admired her wherewithal.

She also had with her a very old cat in a carrier. The cat was long-haired and cantankerous. She reached into the carrier and stroked the cat along the back and neck. The cat murmured contentedly.

"Would you please board Lula until my husband comes home?" she asked. "At least, with Lula here, he won't come home to an empty house. My husband will pay the bill for the dog and the cat when he picks up Lula."

Sunday afternoons the clinic was open from five to six so that people returning from their weekend jaunts could pick up their pets and avoid another overnight fee. This particular Sunday was Stan's and my turn to open the clinic and release animals to their owners. There weren't many animals boarding that weekend, so we anticipated being out of there in relatively short time.

All the clients we were expecting had picked up their pets by five-forty-five. We had had time in between to check that every animal left had water and a clean cage. We were preparing to leave when a Ford Bronco pulled into the parking lot. A clean-cut, nice-looking man in his thirties got out of the car and headed to the front door. He didn't have an animal with him, and he didn't appear in a great hurry. Something didn't seem quite right. He opened the door and came into the reception area.

"Hello," I said, "what can I help you with?"

"I am here to pick up my dog," he said matter-of-factly.

Something in my stomach sank. I knew the animals in the back and who owned them. What was going on here?

"I own Sasha," the man offered. "The well-behaved Vizla."

I didn't know what to do. We hadn't seen another Vizla since the woman came in with the Vizla and Lula, and this man hadn't said a word about a cat named Lula.

"Uh, do you have a cat named Lula?" I asked cautiously.

"Lula!" He made a sound between a choke and a chuckle. "That mangy old cat? I bet she fought to the bitter end, didn't she? I told my wife to put her down months ago, but she refused. I swear, sometimes my wife can be almost as cantankerous as that cat."

I was getting a real bad feeling in the pit of my stomach. How had this happened? How had we euthanized the wrong animal? I was sure we had done exactly as requested.

We had the consent form, didn't we? We had had a discussion about why the dog was being euthanized and why the cat was being boarded.

"I'll be right back," I said, smiling weakly at the man.

Around the corner I quickly ran through the file to find the consent form. There it was. The woman had circled "dog," not cat. She had written in the name "Sasha," not "Lula." She had signed on the line stating that she understood that the animal was to be put to death by lethal injection. The woman had made no mistake.

I hurried to find Stan. We both re-examined the consent form. There was nothing to do but inform the man. Stan called him into the exam room while I went to retrieve Lula in hopes of calming the man with one live animal at least. When I returned to the exam room with Lula growling sullenly from her cat carrier, the man was pacing back and forth, pounding his right fist into the palm of his left hand. The consent form lay on the exam table like an accusation. He looked up when I entered the room.

"What's that?" he said, staring at the cat carrier.

"It's Lula," I replied. At that, he stopped pacing. His face grew red and he threw his arms in the air. Suddenly he turned and sagged onto the bench where he sat, head in his hands, his shoulders heaving up and down.

"I'm sorry," Stan said. "We had no way of knowing. She's been in so many times before. I'm sorry."

It was a long few minutes before the man looked up. He stared at Lula interminably before finally saying, "Do it. And tell me how much I owe you."

As the story unfolded there in the exam room, it became apparent that the policeman had no idea his wife was leaving him while he was at the academy. She had waited until he was gone, then brought his most precious possession, his dog, in to be killed. She had left two things for him: a note taped on Lula's carrier informing him of her intentions and the thing he hated most—Lula—to run up his bill and greet him upon his return. He had returned to a house emptied out and no forwarding address. She had taken everything.

Weekends were something we all looked forward to if we weren't on call. It was a much-needed break from the frantic routine of the week's emergencies, surgeries, and public relations. Doug was not on call, so he was especially looking forward to the weekend. Nothing special was planned for once. Just puttering with the pigeons and falcons, maybe friends out on Sunday evening.

He was enjoying a glass of wine while reading an account of falconry in the United Emerits when he heard the commotion out front. It sounded like someone hitting the breaks hard on gravel which in fact was exactly it. He heard the yip, then doors slamming and excited voices. Before he could put his glass and his book down and get to the window, there was a pounding at the kitchen door.

Doug opened the door and there stood a couple young college kids, their faces framed in tragedy, one of them holding Dinky, the next-door neighbor's Pomeranian. Dinky's left rear leg dangled oddly from his hip, and he was whimpering and shivering even though the day was warm. The kids had not seen Dinky run out to chase their car, but having hit him, they could not run off and leave him, so they had brought him to the closest house. They did not know Doug was a veterinarian.

Doug examined Dinky and knew he had to be taken to the clinic immediately. He called the neighbors but no one was home, so he left a message on their machine explaining the accident and leaving the clinic phone number. Doug took the little dog to the clinic and an x-ray confirmed what he already knew: The leg had to go. Doug prepared for surgery.

Surgery went as well as could be expected. Dinky was now a three-legged Pomeranian and would take time to convalesce and learn to navigate on three legs. The Orvilles were very appreciative of Doug's efforts, perhaps because they knew the dog should not have had free run of the road in the first place, perhaps because Doug had assured them that the surgery and convalescence were free of charge. Everyone but the dog was happy. Doug and Sharon were invited to the neighbor's house for Fourth of July fireworks.

It was only after the dog came home from the hospital that Doug began to notice the change. At first he wasn't sure if he was imagining it or if it was real, but over time he became more and more convinced that Dinky was holding Doug personally responsible for the loss of his left hind limb. It seemed that Dinky noticed whenever Doug came home at night. Dinky would bounce on three legs all the way over to Doug and Sharon's and balance out there barking with revenge.

Doug came to the clinic complaining that he couldn't get any peace with that damned dog out there barking every time he came home. At first the staff thought it was amusing, the idea of this little ball of three-legged fluff, bouncing up and down outside Doug and Sharon's house, trying to hold

Doug accountable the only way it knew how.

We were all convinced that, with time, Dinky would come to terms with his situation and accept it as the norm. He would, if not forgive Doug, at least forget Doug's involvement and get on with more dogly matters.

The night we all went to dinner at the Rose Café, we were in good spirits. The clinic had brought in an all-time record amount of money that day. Business was good. Word was getting out about the new young veterinarian.

Rose Café was one of our favorite places to eat in town. We went to Rose for a sense of community. We knew everyone there. This particular night we were all in a festive mood. As we reviewed the intricacies of the day, Stan asked Doug whether Dinky was still persisting. As soon as Stan asked, something like trouble settled over the table. Sharon rolled her eyes and looked at her plate. Doug laid down his chopsticks and poured himself more tea.

"That dog," Doug began, "is demonic. He not only barks when I pull into the driveway, he barks when there are lights on in the house. He knows when I'm home and as long as I'm there, he won't shut up." The veins in Doug's neck protruded.

"Maybe you should take out a restraining order on him," Stan said, joking.

Sharon didn't laugh, and Doug seemed to perk up at the idea.

The next day Doug came into the office late. Stan had completed three spays before Doug scrubbed up and came into the surgery room.

"I did it," he announced.

"Did what?" Stan asked, his thoughts on his surgery.

"I went to see the sheriff," Doug said matter-of-factly. "I explained the situation and they gave me a restraining order on that little demon."

"You're joking," Stan said, incredulous. "I was only fooling around when I said that."

Doug was not joking. He had explained the story of Dinky's lost leg, the animosity that Dinky had for him, the constant haranguing when he was at home. The sheriff knew Doug was a respectable member of the business community who would not make such an accusation lightly. He had given Doug the restraining order.

By the time Doug got home that evening, it was evident that the neighbors had been informed of Dinky's boundaries. The sheriff had given the neighbors three options: They could keep the dog in the house at all times except for bathroom breaks on a leash; they could have the dog debarked so he could still bark but silently; or they could muzzle him any time he was outdoors. They had gone for the muzzle. When Doug came home, there was Dinky in the middle of the dirt road, muzzled and bouncing up and down on his three legs as fast as he could bounce.

It wasn't long until everyone at the clinic had begun to notice the change. Doug often seemed distracted. He spent much more time at his desk than interacting with people and patients. *Were he and Sharon having trouble*, the staff wondered. Sharon seemed stressed out a lot and both appeared as though they were losing sleep. No one had nerve to ask, however, and it did seem that Doug was confiding in Stan.

The *situation*, as we came to call it, was escalating. According to Doug, Dinky was out of control. The neighbors were not very good about keeping him confined to their own yard, and we had seen for ourselves several instances when the muzzled Dinky came hopping into the yard, only to be swooped up soon after by two terrified-looking little girls.

One evening after work, we all headed to Rose Café for dinner. The topic of conversation quickly turned to the *situation*. It seemed that Dinky no longer needed the sound of a VW bug in the driveway to know Doug was at home. He didn't even need lights on in the house anymore. According to Doug, Dinky could now sense when Doug was at home. The dog could actually distinguish between when Sharon was home alone and when Doug was there. At first it was necessary to keep the blinds pulled so the dog couldn't see light on in the house at night, but now Doug insisted that he and Sharon creep around inside their own house in the dark, blinds pulled. It had gotten to the point that Doug insisted on using subtitles on the television to cut down on the sound. And still Dinky seemed to sense Doug's presence.

As Doug wove this unimaginable tale of a Pomeranian possessed, I noticed that no one at our table was laughing any more. Stan, unaware of the weight of his words, commented that Doug ought to medicate Dinky.

"Give him some *acepromazine* in a little cat food to mellow him out. Dogs love cat food," Stan prescribed.

"I could do better than that," Doug replied. "Let's think a minute. What do we have that won't leave trace in his system?"

As Doug and Stan sat there in the midst of Rose Café planning the demise of the *situation,* I looked cautiously around, wondering who all was overhearing this conversation, who might die of mysterious circumstances overnight, who might report to the police the strange conversation they overheard at the Rose Café the night before, who might come knocking on our door in the wee hours of the morning.

The reports and plans continued in this vein for a few weeks. Doug even built an eight-foot fence between their property and the Orvilles. He thought that would keep Dinky from seeing whether they were at home or not. Once he had the fence up, however, he started worrying about what was happening on the other side of the fence, so he very carefully drilled a tiny peephole in order to watch what was going on on the other side. We all began to feel badly for Doug. After a few days of peeping through the hole, Doug had begun to think he needed more peepholes, strategically placed, in order to watch from all angles. Sharon was worried. The lines around her eyes were more pronounced and the set of her mouth was tighter than ever before.

One Saturday Sharon invited us out for burgers on the grill. She thought a little friendly get-together in the light of day might lift Doug's spirits. At the very least, it would be a relief for her to have someone else to talk with about something other than that dog.

We arrived and found Doug poking the charcoal around in the pit. He seemed in better spirits than we had seen in weeks. Dinky was not around either. Another good sign. The early evening was calm and the only sound was the pigeons cooing from the pen. I went in the house to join Sharon while Stan stayed outside with Doug.

Sharon and I each grabbed a glass of chardonnay from the kitchen and headed toward the hot tub room. From there we could visit, compare notes on Doug and Dinky, and gossip good-naturedly while watching what was going on outside with the grilling. We were just about through our first glass of wine when we saw Doug and Stan jump into the VW bug, slam the doors, and turn that car on a quarter as it peeled out of the gravel driveway.

The hot tub room was all glass, so we watched in the direction of the trail of dust they left behind. They had not headed toward town but in the opposite direction down the gravel road. We were sitting there when back the Beetle came, again racing into the yard. Doug jumped out of the car and ran toward the house.

Doug hurried into the house and headed straight for the basement. A moment later he was up the stairs, a rifle in hand, as he headed back to the Bug.

There was nothing for Sharon or me to do but wait. We knew this was it—Dinky's demise. All those discussions about poisons over dinner were behind us. No poison. No planning. In the blink of an eye, a glimpse of insanity had hijacked the evening.

Doug and Stan were gone a bit longer this time, but when they did come back, they drove into the driveway, parked the car, and calmly got out and headed toward the house. Doug went straight to the basement and reappeared without the rifle. He and Stan set about grilling the burgers. Sharon and I prepared the rest of the meal. We ate at the dining table looking out over the meadow, watching as the sun burned its path across the horizon. Doug was subdued as we ate. Stan was over-solicitous. Sharon and I were cautious, aware of the unharnessed electricity in the air.

Dinner did not last late into the evening. We cleaned up the dishes, thanked Doug and Sharon and said something about early morning surgeries. On the way home, I asked Stan for the story.

"You won't believe it," he said. "I can hardly believe it myself."

"What happened?" I urged. "Doug shot Dinky, didn't he?"

"No," Stan nodded, "it didn't happen that way."

"What do you mean? We saw him with the gun!"

"Yeah, well, we saw Dinky head down the road away from all the houses, and Doug suggested we just follow him a bit, you know, just *give Dinky something to think about*, as Doug put it."

"Something to *think* about? Did he shoot him or didn't he?" I demanded.

"I think that was the plan, but then Dinky ran into a culvert back there under the road, and Doug chased after him with the gun in tow, but then he bent down and looked in the culvert and there was Dinky, cowering back in the shadows and shaking.

"Doug raised the gun to his shoulder and Dinky was whimpering, and I thought Doug was starting to take mercy on the poor thing. I saw Doug lay the gun down on the ground and get down on his knees in front of the culvert. I thought he was going to try to coax Dinky out and take him home."

"Did he take him home?" I asked.

"No. I thought he was going to but then I saw him reach for a big rock nearby. I watched as he dragged and pushed that rock until he had it in front of the culvert. Then he ran around to the other end and found another rock. When he was done, he stood up and brushed off his hands and his pants and smiled the biggest smile I have seen on his face in months."

"You left him there inside the culvert?" I asked. Stan's face darkened.

"*I* couldn't do anything. Doug would have been furious if I had tried. You see how he is. Are *you* going to stop him?"

I felt sick to my stomach. How could my own husband tolerate this? Doug had entombed the three-legged dog in the culvert. He had decided, he confided in Stan, to go visit Dinky daily, to watch his imprisoned demon perish slowly, as slowly, he said, as Dinky had tortured him over the past months, barking and bouncing in the lane.

The rest of the drive home was a silent one. We spent the remainder of the evening escaping in front of the television. I went to bed early and barely noticed when Stan joined me several hours later. I did notice, however, around three in the morning when Stan crawled from the bed and began to get dressed. I didn't ask what he was doing. I pretended to sleep.

He was gone for no more than an hour. When he got back in bed, he whispered, "Dinky's free." He rolled away from me, and we comforted ourselves each in our own bit of darkness.

The next morning we prepared to go to the clinic.

"Does Doug know?" I asked.

"No," Stan responded. "When I got to the lane, I turned off my headlights and drove quietly past until I got to the area. Then I used a flashlight to find the culvert in the dark. I just rolled one rock away and Dinky didn't waste any time getting out of there. Last I saw, he was bouncing toward home, and I didn't stick around to see if he made it."

We went to work that morning filled with trepidation. If Doug saw Dinky, we knew there would be consequences. On the other hand, maybe he too had come to his senses by morning and would be glad to see Dinky bouncing and muzzled out front. Maybe we would all be laughing over lunch about the crazy events of the night before.

Doug and Sharon were late coming in to work. Sharon came in first.

"You shouldn't have done that," was all she said and went to work on the payroll.

When Doug did come in, he went directly to his office and shut the door without speaking to anyone. The staff was wide-eyed and curious. Everyone seemed to understand that there was something serious going on between Doug and Stan but they didn't know what. Everyone on staff knew we were all good friends.

The days and weeks passed and things did not get better between the two doctors. Each did their job and spent the rest of their time avoiding each other. Staff didn't chat in the main office anymore. Everyone kept busy filing, autoclaving, cleaning, anything to avoid chit chat.

The clinic was polished to a shine, but there remained a nagging static in the wiring that made the electricity flicker from time to time. It hadn't become a problem yet, but Stan thought he knew what the problem was and he thought he could fix it. Early one morning before Doug and Sharon arrived, Stan turned off the power. He personally told each and every person that he was going to the attic to work on the wiring and *no one* was to turn the power back on until he came down and did it himself.

Stan climbed into the attic with his toolbox and began to work on the wiring. He quickly spotted where the problem lay, isolated the offending wires, and reached for the wire cutter. To his irritation he realized he had set the toolbox just slightly out of his own reach without letting go of the wires he had isolated. He let go and stretched to pull the toolbox closer to his work. Just as he turned away, the power suddenly came on. The wires sparked. Then the wires went dead. The power was off. Stan knelt there in the heat of the attic shivering.

He was angry. Who would have been so careless as to turn on the power? He had gone around to every single person and given them instructions himself. And then he heard a noise outside like someone stepping on the rotting wood below the windowsill. He moved to the window just in time to see Doug turning away and heading back toward the rear entrance.

Whereas before, people gathered around the coffee pot in the mornings and reviewed the day's events, now people poured their coffee and disappeared to their own nook of the clinic. Stan stopped drinking coffee altogether unless he brought in his own cup and made instant coffee from hot tap water. He would not eat anything brought into the clinic.

This was like the worst imaginable divorce. The whole clinic was suffering. The staff loved both doctors and could not understand how their relationship could have soured so badly.

Stan was beside himself with worry. He had thought we would live out our lives here in this community. He worried about his job, about house payments, about his reputation. He couldn't sleep. He scarcely ate. I decided to take our son to visit his grandparents while Stan figured out our next move.

One morning I awoke to the smell of bacon and hot coffee. The sun was shining and robins were chirping. I could hear Jason making train sounds with his granddad. I realized there were no knots in my shoulders. We were a world away from chaos.

I could hear the radio's litany of morning happenings around the state. Rodeos and parades around the state, something about a sale of wild horses, controversy over wolves versus ranchers in Montana, a dinosaur dig in the Bighorns, murder in southern Wyoming. Did I hear correctly?

"Did you hear the news?" my mother asked the moment I entered the kitchen.

"No, I haven't," I lied.

"You didn't hear about the murder?" Mother said.

About that time the phone rang. It was Stan. I could hear the excitement in his voice immediately. Doug and Sharon's neighbor had been drinking. He came home and was abusive to his wife, only this time, she had had enough. She, the girls, and Dinky were packing up. She was tired of the feud. She was leaving.

At her announcement, Orville had reached over and grabbed the .38 special out of the bureau drawer. Before she could react, he had shot her dead. The news described the little girls found huddling at the scene, clutching their Pomeranian, shivering. Orville was on the run and there was an all points bulletin out on him. Doug, Stan explained, was fit to be tied. Doug was sure Orville was coming after him next. Sharon had confided in Stan that Doug had brought the rifle up from the basement and sat in the living room with the rifle aimed at the front door. She was fearful if Orville didn't get them, Doug's own paranoia would.

It was only a matter of hours, however, until Orville's brother walked Orville into the sheriff's office, and he turned himself in. Orville went to trial and was sentenced to twenty-five years in the state penitentiary. The little girls and Dinky went to live with their aunt and uncle.

Doug, however, had turned a different corner and could not return. He was convinced that Orville would spend his days in prison plotting the day he would get released and could come after him. Doug no longer seemed to remember that Dinky was the one with the grudge. Doug sold the clinic to an out-of-towner shortly after Orville was convicted. He bought tickets to somewhere in the Middle East where it is rumored he lives to this day, working on falcons and camels, chief veterinarian of sheiks. No matter all the past quirks of the kaleidoscope. Who is to say, after all, what disturbs that fragile balance we think of as sanity? Perhaps it is nothing more than a matter of perspective.

GETTING FRANK

I don't recall just when my father gave up the game of hunting, but he stopped sometime in mid-life. Maybe about the same time he gave up smoking. He put the guns away, hidden so deeply in the bowels of the house, I never ran into them again. In their place, he took up painting. He painted landscapes, still lifes, bull fights, rodeos, and trains. He copied old masters to see what he could learn, but the thing that he did best was portraits. Slowly, over time he captured most of the town. He captured Bruce Kennedy, the local newspaperman and town philosopher in his wire-rimmed spectacles, and Oscar Shoemaker, the kindly, humpbacked florist with the Hitler mustache and the warm brown eyes. He captured the rancher's daughter, costumed in her Miss Wyoming regalia, and the German teacher with her long, blonde hair loose, her shoulder skirting exposure. He captured Felix the sheepherder, his wrinkled face a topography of Basque migration. He even captured the local priests, first Monsignor McBride, and then, he got the Bishop too. More recently, the heads of the newer priests of the diocese bedeck the wall. It keeps his eye honed, hunting down those little quirks that lead one man down a particular path or another.

One painting in particular disturbs me. It is of a man wearing a lightly faded, blue shirt. He wears a wide-brimmed hat pulled low which casts a broad, dark shadow over his eyes, making it difficult to get a look at his face. The light blue shirt becomes sky and fades into another vignette. A man is riding a horse through the desert, pauses at a dwindling water hole. There is something about the man that seems familiar to me, yet I cannot put my finger on it. Do I know him? I do not recognize him, but at the same time, I think I do recognize him. Is he a long-lost relative I have seen in photos? I ask my father who he is, where he spotted the man, and do I know this man.

My father of few words replied, "He's nobody special. He's just someone inside my own head."

I pushed on, determined to track down this man's identity. "What is he doing?" I asked.

My father furrowed his brow.

"Is he hunting?" I say, becoming badger.

He shuffled a foot.

"Where is he going?"

He scratched his head.

Why can't I see his eyes?" I prodded.

Then finally, after an interminable pause, he pursed his lips and said, "He's just an old man. He's an old desert rat who lives out there in the badlands somewhere."

"But how does he live?" I pursued. "Where does he get food and money?"

By now my father had decided the only way out was straight ahead. "He has enough to get along," my father said. "He doesn't need much. He knows where to find what he needs."

"What about money?" I pressed. "Doesn't he need money?"

"He probably has a little stash of gold out there in the brush somewhere." My father began to fidget, uncomfortable in the barrage of questions. "When he needs it, he knows where to find it."

"What about his eyes? Why doesn't he have eyes?"

"He has eyes," my father assured me. "They may be hidden by the shadow of his hat, and you may not be able to see his eyes," he said quietly, "but he has eyes, and he sees you just fine."

I fidgeted, suddenly feeling as if scrutiny had turned on me and hit me right between the eyes. I quickly left this path of questions behind.

Over the years, my father had used me for a model. He started painting me when I was in adolescence. I was flattered to be a real artist's model and took great care to paint my face and choose my clothes for posterity. I teased my hair high and sprayed it. I sat upright, my chin slightly out, my shoulders squared, my hands carefully draped on my lap, a gesture, I thought, of gentility. I assumed my most practiced Giaconda smile. I envisioned myself, years hence, gilded with gold and peering down upon those who came after me. I thought I might become the famous *Girl with Pout* or perhaps, *Perfection in Repose*. For as much effort as I put into being the most exquisite model of youthful perfection, I could never understand how my father, a generally recognized local artist, could never capture me. My nose was too abrupt. My smile a little crooked. My posture was rigid and my eyes too disconnected from my surroundings. *What was his problem?*

I now own most of those early portraits. They are as I remembered them. My nose is indeed stuck in the air, my mouth a permanent pout. I am most definitely not the next Mona Lisa, and my eyes are less dreamy now. I recall my father's comment that he didn't like to paint young women. Their character, he said, was yet to show wrinkles.

I wince to think that my father was better at revealing character, or lack thereof, than I care to admit. He did not have a formal art education. He attended Business College and became a railroader, a good paying occupation with good benefits. Some of my earliest memories, however, are of him working at his easel out on the lawn under the cottonwood trees, his pallet smeared with blues, white, black, yellow. Every now and then he would pause and gaze off. I always wondered what he saw as he painted. Could he see things in the clouds that I could not? Years later I ran across a photo in an album my mother had put together. In this photo my father sits, a handsome young rogue at his easel under the cottonwoods, pipe dangling from his lip, his brush frozen in midair before the image of Christ that had somehow emerged from the clouds just above our cottonwoods.

Although my father did not have a formal art education, he read art books voraciously. He sought out the artists in whatever community he found himself. He visited art museums. It was not uncommon to find my father examining items as closely as possible. I saw him jiggle an emerald on a crown in a palace in Germany. I once saw him lie face down on his stomach on a polished marble floor, right at the feet of a guard, in order to look up underneath a porcelain oven of sorts *to see how it works*. The guard did nothing. I guess he figured no thief in his right mind would be so blatant. In Italy, while poring over the works of the old masters in a local church, the church bells suddenly started tolling and people started filing in, genuflecting, and taking their seats for prayer. My mother and I thought perhaps we should leave before the service, and she whispered to me, "Go find your father," but I did not have to look far. Around the corner in the bell tower stood my father, straining with every pull on the heavy rope that rang the bell. *Had he summoned the faithful?*

I thought our whole family might be arrested in Amsterdam, or at the very least, deported when we visited the Rijksmuseum. My father would lean as far over the security rope as balance could possibly support. He had such a knack for finding the space with the least distance between him and a painting that I usually tried not to be in the same room with him. It was too stressful. It was also predictable when, to my horror, alarms starting ringing and guards starting rushing into the room where Rembrandt's *Nightwatch* hung surrounded by rope and wired carpet. The guards were all business and their hands rested lightly on their holsters. Both my mother and I rushed toward the ruckus, but my father was nowhere to be found. He was in an adjoining room, sitting rapt on a couch peering at a DaVinci Madonna, while a woman who had stepped on the carpet in front of *Nightwatch* was led gruffly away.

The railroad was what afforded our family a comfortable lifestyle. The railroad, along with my mother's teaching salary, made it possible for our family to travel. We took several trips by car deep into Mexico. When we arrived in Morelia, we would go to the *mercado* and let the word get out that *"Francisco Cortez, hermano de Julio del Norte, esta en la ciudad!"* and wait for the old aunts, as we called them, to hunt us down. To get to my relatives' villages we had to drive into the country and park the car, then hike back in, climbing over rock walls along the way. The whole village would turn out to greet us. My father was a local hero it seemed, the nephew who lived "up north" and made it rich but who still came back to visit the aunts. Our car was always a major point of interest, as most of the relatives either walked or rode horseback. Feasts were held in my father's honor and he would be asked to resolve the family disputes while there. As a child I thought we must be Mexican royalty, but what had happened to the family wealth? Why did people live in two-room houses with dirt floors, and why was there no furniture, only raw timber chairs and a table? Why were there no roads to drive on? How was my life connected to these people?

The ironies of such a life as my father's must have been even more notable to him. He remembered living in half a boxcar in Kansas. He remembered following the railroad tracks north when at age five he ran away from his parents who had returned to Mexico to visit. He remembered a lot more than he ever shared with his daughters. It was my mother who gave bits and pieces of the past to us. She told us how late one night some Mexican friends in a neighboring Kansas community had come knocking frantically at the door of my grandfather. It seems the Ku Klux Klan was planning on running the Mexicans out of town, and my grandfather's gun was needed for protection. I didn't hear how that night turned out, but it must not have gone well for the Mexicans. Many years later when my father was retired and spending leisurely winters in Arizona, he ran into a man living in the same retirement community who remembered that earlier Kansas evening.

"Remember the night we ran the Mexicans out of town?" the man reminisced, happy to run into someone from the good ol' days.

Life is full of irony. One boy started his journey from a boxcar; one boy grew up in a house with a front porch swing. One boy's father couldn't speak English; one boy's father owned his own business. Both boys, in their late seventies, ultimately arrived in Arizona, a state populated with Mexicans, at the same potlucks in the same winter retirement complex.

My father may have started from humble background, but his real quality made him rise in the estimation of all who knew him. As a boy in southeastern

Kansas, he became the star point guard of the basketball team. He was short but fast and a sharp study. He had moves the taller boys couldn't match, as well as an accurate eye, and he led the team to two championship years. When his father had to move in order to keep his job with the railroad, it was the town doctor who asked if Frank could stay to play basketball for the town. It was arranged. Frank's father needed a character reference to take with him to the neighboring town. The good doctor would write the letter, and Frank would remain in Benedict. He would stay with the doctor's sister, a school teacher. They would eat dinner with the doctor's family where Frank would learn to love gravy, that great midwestern delicacy. He would go on to play ball. He would remain the secret weapon of Benedict, Kansas. The reference letter came to me recently via my mother. It was dated August 18, 1936, and read: *This is to certify that we have known Julio Cortez for 10 years and can say he is honest in every way and a worker; he is our Mexican who was always ready at any time to work.* It was signed by B. R. Riley, M.D., and four other men of the Benedict basketball promoters. Frank's ticket to upward mobility.

When the boys all went swimming at the local water hole, he was the one swinging wide on a rope, far out over the mossy green water, fish jumping as though he might be the prize if they could just jump a little higher. But in the end it was he, the alpha male as usual, who nabbed the prize, my mother, who also hung around the watering hole on hot summer Kansas days.

In spite of his family's struggles, Frank found leisure time for his creative side. There was a small circus that wintered in Benedict when he was around twelve, and Frank and the boys often made pocket change by helping to feed and clean up after the animals. One day he and the doctor's kids got the idea to put on their own circus and charge kids in the neighborhood to attend. They built a trapeze out of saw-horses and rope, and one boy billed himself as the trapeze artist as he balanced precariously. One boy dressed up like a clown. One put the family cat in a wooden orange crate which they had painted to look like a wild tiger's cage, then provoked the cat until it growled ferociously. One bribed the dog with sausages to get it to jump through a hoop. The doctor's daughter wanted to be the magician's assistant. Then Frank had an idea. He was very athletic and had a keen eye to boot. They could get the neighborhood kids to pay more if they could promise something spectacular. He would bill himself as *Frank the Fearless, knife thrower extraordinaire*, and the doctor's daughter could be his assistant! He could paint on a mustache and goatee and attach a towel for a cloak. He knew where the doctor had a bunch of old scalpels for use in the barn. They would be perfect.

The big event would be held inside the doctor's barn. They painted a location for the doctor's daughter to stand. As my father told me one day when reminiscing, "Martha Ellen would stand very quietly in front of her prescribed spot, and I am sure she held her breath as I very carefully tossed the 'knives' so as to *just* miss her. Not once did I knick her flesh, and the two or three audience members got their money's worth. There was an old x-ray machine in the attic of the barn, so give us credit for not taking x-rays of people too!"

One can only wonder how he convinced the doctor's daughter to be his assistant as he practiced throwing scalpels. What charm he must have exuded as he talked that little girl into standing motionless against the barn while he drew a bead on points around her head, and all the boys, including her brother, stood mesmerized as they watched in absolute silence as Frank threw the doctor's scalpels. How did he do this? How did he get her to stand there, pitch after fateful pitch? How did he miss her? And where did they all find such utter faith? He was the best knife thrower in southeastern Kansas. He was the point guard of Benedict. He was everybody's trophy.

Class and culture sometimes make strange bedfellows, and yet it is said that opposites attract. Everybody wanted young Frank. Everybody admired his talents and his wit. Yet, there were those who would have his family run out of town if they could. And while he was a dashing young man, all that dash would lead to clash when he fell in love with my mother. (Her father, my grandfather, is said to have belonged to the Ku Klux Klan in southeastern Kansas and while her father was organizing rallies, his father, my paternal grandfather, was being threatened by the Klan in a nearby community!) If it hadn't been for all that charm, young Frank might have found himself in deep water when he began to pay notice to Emma Grace Usher. But when he cleaned out her desk, leaving her books piled on the floor, and moved into her seat, instead of feeling threatened, she was flattered. It wasn't long before she was sneaking out to the swimming hole to watch Frank and his buddies carouse and hold court.

While my parents never said much about the opposition my maternal grandparents afforded, I did grow up knowing that my parents had eloped from Kansas to Wyoming to get married. I heard the stories of how they only had ten dollars to start up housekeeping, how they got hired to work in the fields at one farmer or another's place. Everything I heard seemed to come in late night whispers or shadows of innuendo. Things like how Mrs. Everett invited Grace to have lunch in the dining room with the family but told Frank to eat out behind the barn. Lying in bed late at night, I still remember the unfathomed pride I felt tingling up my spine to the base of my neck when my mother told this story in the adjoining room, and I would hear the indignation rise powerful in her voice as she declined such incivility and chose the more gracious companionship of the chickens, the barn cats, and my father. This must have been but a taste of the discrimination my father endured back then, but I never heard him speak of it. There must have been plenty of stories but my father did not dwell upon them. My father had a vision that took up his whole field of sight.

He saw a world that would not deny his three young daughters. As a young child I was encouraged to explore, to imagine, to read and write and play school. I had what all children in my town had in the nineteen fifties. I had a normal childhood but enhanced. I had what the others had but I had one more thing that even my sisters did not have--my father's time. Because he was my babysitter while my mother taught school, I had him all to myself. I got to absorb him. If he ate sardines, I ate sardines. I hiked where he hiked. I twitched when he twitched and my head itched when he scratched. I followed him around town on his errands, listening to his banter with the other men at the elevator, the co-op, the post office, and the depot. I saw without noticing how the men deferred to my father.

As I grew older, I became more aware of my father's hold on our town. I knew I was a *Cortez Girl*. It was sort of like being a *Ziegfried Girl*, I suppose. It meant I was going to be noticed. It also meant that I was expected to be a model child. *Cortez Girls* were smart, well-mannered, well-traveled. *Cortez Girls* could not date just any boy. Could not attend most parties. And I was the youngest. I was expected to have ironed out all the wrinkles. And any little wrinkle that surfaced in my behavior found its way back to my father. The worst part of slippage was that the wrinkle showed up on my father's forehead, and the pain of my slip could be heard in his voice. *Cortez*, I understood, was not a name to wear lightly.

And so it was with great excitement in August of 2001, that it was announced my father was to have a retrospective of his life's work at the Art Shelter Studio Gallery in Shell, Wyoming. The reception would take place on September fifteenth. He would show oils, acrylics, and watercolors. He would show mountain scenes, railroad scenes, American Indians, and portraits. He would fill four rooms with his works. Frank was a town treasure. Many had seen his works here or there but never so many in one place. And to see all the portraits! Who all had he captured?

His portraits were viewed as something of a *Who's Who* list of Greybull. You had made it if you had been painted by Frank. Everyone wanted to see whom Frank had stashed in that studio of his. He had a whole collection of people and hadn't, up till now at least, turned many of them loose. *Felix* and *Oscar* would be there, of course, but the *Desert Rat* was in Kansas as was his *Orphan*. *Geronimo* would be there as well as *Onisimo*, painted for Barry Goldwater's collection had Barry not died. And of course, all the priests and the Bishop would be there. The grand ladies Frank saw on his travels would bump shoulders with the wranglers who were well-represented, even the boys just learning to chew. The two bullfighters from Spain would wave their capes as my Great-Great Uncle Hezekiah the Scalawag looked over the crowd as if wondering how to turn a profit when my father had placed a *Not for Sale* sign on his waistcoat. A *Cortez Girl* looked dreamily on as a young scout counted coup, and the family rooster stood fluffed and crowing, royal and possessive as a temple lion.

My husband and I were flying in for the event. My son was flying from Boston. My sister and husband were driving from South Dakota. We would see people we had not seen in thirty years. I realized I was going to become a *Cortez Girl* once again. I shopped. I primped. I worried. Should I really try for that old aura, or should I settle more gracefully into middle-aged efficiency? Efficiency was certainly more comfortable these days. I could plan and prepare the reception. I could wear black and look mysterious instead of shy in my silence. I could watch everything, gather the quirks for later, as people milled from room to room, my father more fluffed and proud in his quiet way than that bantam rooster on the wall.

It was much more than a mere art exhibition and though no one said so, everyone seemed to know it. It was to be a kind of unspoken inauguration. A town acknowledgment, of sorts, for the wrongs of the past. There would be people there from the early days of the sugar beet fields, those who ate behind the barn with him and those who didn't. There would be men who broke the same sweat with him as they toiled over heavy old engines from the round house days, and Greybull's upper crust women from the business community who wanted to study art in Frank's presence. No matter one's politics, Frank was now the candidate of choice. While he could never be coerced into running for mayor, much as they tried, he did serve on the Seniors' Board of Directors, and he reached the top level in the Knights of Columbus. He was the county translator for all Latinos hauled into court, justly or otherwise. I liked to think they saw a little more humanity because of him. Although he never spoke of the injustices he had endured, I knew he felt them deeply. This was made clear to me when out of the blue one day I received in the mail a packet of clippings he had carefully annotated. There was a racist rambling from a local newspaper about *wetbacks multiplying like roaches sharing rent and food and stealing the jobs of honest, hard-working Americans*. There was an article from the *Casper Star Tribune* about the police in Jackson Hole, Wyoming, who rounded up the Mexicans in town and corralled them by herding them into a fenced parking lot adjacent to the Teton County Jail until their immigration status could be checked by INS and it could be determined who was legal and who wasn't. The Teton County Sheriff was quoted in the article saying that *skin color was absolutely a sufficient reason to stop, question, and detain a suspected illegal alien.* There was a story about a Mexican-American girl, born and raised in the U.S., rounded up and dumped far enough across the border to discourage her from finding her way back, never mind that she couldn't even speak Spanish. This was as close as he ever came to sharing with me the hurt and pain, and yes, his fear for me, of the bigotry that he himself had experienced. It was a kind of cautionary tale for me. He seemed to be telling me that I may be well-educated and far too assimilated for my own liking, I may be *Cortez Girl* through and through, but in the eyes of some, I will always be first cousin to cockroach. It is because of those that I must always be vigilant.

This lesson was brought home to me personally on September 12, 2001, the day after Al Quaeda flew planes into the World Trade Center and changed all American lives hence. We had watched with horror the events unfolding on our television screens, yet it was difficult to absorb the reality of the event. While I knew this horrendous thing was happening on the East Coast, I still could not understand that we would not be able to board a plane in Kansas City and fly to Wyoming for my father's show. It was incomprehensible to me that people could hate so hard. I thought my son might experience delays in trying to leave Boston, but surely he could fly to Wyoming. After all, Wyoming wasn't Washington.

Kansas City was an occupied country when we arrived there early for our flight. Everything was hushed and no one was belligerent. That was the most frightening thing—that donned complicit civility—seemed to suggest that we all knew how tenuous was our hold on our world, that we were right on the brink of chaos, and just one wrong word might send us hurdling over the edge of the abyss.

I stepped to the counter to inquire about our flight. They were the friendliest agents I have ever encountered, but big and not used to working the keyboards. They were *very sorry, ma'am,* **(Who says "ma'am" in KANSAS?)**, *but you will not be flying to Wyoming, not today, not tomorrow, not any day any time soon. And no, ma'am, your son most definitely won't be leaving Boston. Looks like none of you is going to make it to God's country. Boston, that's where those camel-jockeys commandeered those planes from. Don't know what they're doing here in America any way; damn camel-jockeys should all go back where they come from.*

And the words of warning in my father's clippings turned to liquid fear that flooded my veins. Why is this smiling man saying this to me? Why is he calling Arabs *camel-jockeys*? Can he look on the monitor and tell that my son, trying to leave Boston the day after chaos, has Arabic blood in his veins? Does it matter? Today does it matter? I have never feared for his safety because of the blood in his veins, my son, the United Nations. If a crime lab analyzed his blood, could they recognize the Irish, the Welsh, the Mexican mix of Spanish and Indigenous from me, the German, the English, and Arabic from his father? Could they weigh the quantity? Mexican and Arab would be greatest. *Two parts cockroach? Is this what the man at the counter is seeing on his screen?*

And I feel sick to my stomach. Now I understand the swirling bile in the abyss. My father had tried to warn me. It's always there. It's always been there, lingering behind the sweet smile of acceptance. I've seen it myself in some professor's face when I've intervened for a student. I've rubbed noses with it over cocktails. I have smelled it billowing up in the reluctant acquiescence of supervisors. I have heard it in the patronizing sing-song of a colleague who just made a "prize hire": *I got me a Mexican!* I taste it now as I write these acrid words, but *cockroach! Cockroach* suddenly is transformed!

Cockroach is quick. It scuttles. It thrives in spite of decomposition. My son is safe. He knows how to blend in. He fits wherever he is, but still I know he must learn. He must not think these parts of him do not exist, that these parts of him do not matter. They are what he is, and he will grow into them as he learns more about bigotry in the world, and on September twelve, the world was closing in. He was living in occupied America, occupied by Arabs who hated him for his American blood and Americans who hated him for his Arabic blood. He could not go to God's country. He could not get to Frank.

In Wyoming, however, the skies were clear and blue. The air was crisp. It was mid-September in the Bighorns, and the Twin Towers disaster seemed as distant and strange as King Kong. The town was abuzz. Should the show go on? Should it be cancelled? What was the American thing to do? As the town polling came in, it was unanimous. The American thing to do was to have the show. *Show those Arab camel jockeys they can't dictate the lives of the good people in God's country,* the airline agent would surely agree.

My father held his own counsel. He felt the dust and debris of New York City streets dry in his throat, and he ached through and through. He had always wanted to see New York, that metropolis of world culture. *World power.* He felt shame as he came face-to-face with the Arab terrorists, clothed in his own bigotry, his real hate of Wyoming's sons, Allen Simpson and Dick Cheney, both powerbrokers for the privileged few. He was ashamed. He understood the hate of our attackers. He understood humiliation and degradation and how it could get to you and eat away at the inside of you. He recognized the elements of terrorist.

And then he knew. The show had to go on. The town needed art. Now more than ever before, the town needed humanizing. They all needed Frank. They needed the wranglers, the rivers, the priests and the ponds, the show girls, the trains, the mountains, the roosters, the skies. They needed all of humanity, and on September fifteenth, all of the town's humanity flocked through the door. It was chaos. Farmers and bankers, carpenters and Christians, teachers and grocers, young up-starts and old veterans all came out to the show. They nibbled on cheese and popped grapes till they were giddy. They drank the place dry. They snapped photos with Frank, and they argued over what and who could be bought that night. They all wanted something, some token, before it was over.

And through it all, Frank wandered calmly and quietly, here and there, making friendly small talk and putting everyone at ease. By the end of the evening many paintings had been purchased for far less than he could have made for any one of them. One of those farmer's wives was overheard in the receiving line as she chirped over a painting of an old decomposing barn, "Oh, I have always wanted to get a Frank!"

When my father was a young hunter, his buddies around town called him *One Shot*. He never wasted a bullet. As I write this today, my father is eighty-six years old. If he finds a spider in the house, he carefully scoops it up onto a newspaper and transports it gently outdoors where he releases it in the bushes. In the fall when spiders build their webs in inconvenient pathways, my father will take the long way around to avoid damaging the web. He prefers wandering the hills these days without armor. When I go home to visit, we still like to drive the back roads, our eyes canvassing the fields at the foot of the Bighorns. Occasionally we will scare up a pheasant caught unawares by something as innocuous as a minivan. Then we know we have had a good day. My father has taught me to understand what the poet Wallace Stevens had to say: *Poetry is a pheasant disappearing into the brush.* He understands that a fleeting glimpse of beauty is too rare a thing to pack home in a canvas bag. And the fleeting glimpses of beauty we find in the furrowed faces that greet us are all there is and enough.

SACRED REMAINS

Greybull Standard editorial, July 29, 2004:

Frank and Grace Cortez' auction was a hoot. Many bargains were had, as were a few of the bidders. I suspect many local bidders ran up the price so Frank and Grace would have a nice nest egg for their retirement in Kansas. They deserve as much.

Others simply wanted something and didn't care a hang about the price they paid. A few bidders went home quite disappointed... (Frank) was pleased to some extent in the knowledge that most of his work went to locals who will care for them and pass them to their family members. Perhaps some of his works will be worth a fortune fifty years from now. I hope so: He deserves the immortality.

The day before the carnival the trucks moved in. They set up big open-sided tents, one in the front yard, a second in the back. Fliers had been placed all over town and for sixty miles or more in every direction. Notices were in the local papers, but the best advertising seemed to pass from grocery aisle to post office steps to coffee shop. In Wyoming where nearby towns are thirty to fifty miles apart, the news seemed to spread like pollen on the wind. Anticipation settled in over the towns nestled down in the badlands.

For a full week before the event, a steady flow of vehicles could be seen from sun-up to sun-down cruising slowly down the alley as though it were a main thoroughfare. The phone rang off the hook, and the drapes had to be kept pulled tight to prevent some of the more courageous folks from peering through the windows. Some would come to the front door and ring the doorbell to ask for an early preview or sell: *Say, Frank, I see you've got a riding lawn mower there. How much you take for me to get it off your hands right now?*

I had traveled from Kansas a month in advance to help pack up and clean out. I had no idea what awaited me. Sixty-four years worth of lives lived, struggles endured, victories large and small. My first evening home my mother said, "Go get a box out of the closet and let's go through it."

Dutifully, I went to the designated closet and pulled out the first of many boxes to come not only from that closet but from other closets, from under beds, inside cabinets, down in the basement, out in the two garages, from the shed, and from the studio. I was about to make the acquaintance of my parents.

As youngest daughter in a family of three daughters, I had been sheltered by my parents. Through my childhood lens, we had always had enough money for most anything. We had traveled extensively throughout the United States, deeply into Mexico and across Canada, and spent a whole summer traveling in Europe. My mother was a beloved fourth grade teacher before retirement at the age of fifty-seven, and my father, a railroader, had achieved the highest order of the Knights of Columbus. My parents were well-respected members of the community.

I opened the first box eagerly. My mother's treasures. It was a bit like playing "dress up" as a child when I would go through Mother's jewelry and hats, trying on her high heel shoes, helping myself to her belongings in order to become her for an imaginary moment. Inside the larger box were many smaller boxes of varying dimensions. I opened the first one. It contained cards for every holiday from the year 1952. I was a toddler then. There were birthday wishes from someone named Maxine, Christmas wishes from Junior and family, get-wells and wish-you-were-heres. First names only. No handwritten message on most. Just the given name as though those relationships were so strongly bound, the ties could never be in question.

Cleaning out, I thought, *is going to be easy. No one in his or her right mind would want to save this stuff!* But my mother and father thought differently. As I started to toss a whole yarn-tied bundle into the trash can beside my chair, both of my parents shrieked, their faces etched with horror.

"Stop!" my mother exclaimed. "Let me see those first!" Thus went the first evening of my trip home. Box after box. From cards to clothes-pin Rudolphs made by some unknown fourth-grader to half empty Avon bottles. There were dime store brooches of glittery paste jewelry to broken-bladed pocket knives. Girl Scout pins and perfect attendance stars, my sister's sophomore year diary, all of which my parents had carefully saved all these years, certain each item would be valued by their daughters one day.

This is the way guilt seeps in. Children never understand how much they are loved. We break our parents' hearts over and over again without so much as a shrug. We beg and plead and manipulate until we get that *must-have*, and never realize the true cost in extra hours worked or the exhaustion that comes by early evening. How do you tell a mother who saved to buy your Brownie Scout dress, who washed, ironed, and starched it, who sewed each merit badge carefully in place according to the handbook guidelines, who saved those merit badges since you were eight that forty-seven years later you don't care about them? Instead, you slip them into your pocket with a weak smile and know that she knows you plan to toss them just out of her sight. You feel a little diminished. She is growing visibly smaller before your very eyes.

And the cleaning out continues, day after day, box after box. Nestled in cotton, a smooth gray stone rests. *Another easy decision,* I think to myself.

"Let me see that," my mother says. She takes the stone in the palm of her hand and turns it over. Her face fights a moment for composure.

"I want you to keep this," she tells me as she hands the box over to me.

I pick up the stone. It fits perfectly in the palm of my hand. It is polished smooth but the edges look whittled, almost chipped away like an arrowhead, but shaped like a heart. On one side, scratched into the stone, it reads, "F. C. + G. U." Frank Cortez plus Grace Usher. On the other side it reads, "I love U."

"If you ever need a little something," Mother tells me, "you can find it inside the stone. Your father split the stone and put a dime inside, so as long as you have his heart, you will know you have a little something extra."

After a few days we discovered the best routine. Each of us would take a room to work on alone. That way no one would see what decisions another made. At first I was hesitant to dive into my parents' closets and belongings, but there was so much to go through after sixty-four years. I pulled a cigar box out of my mother's linens. The box had been covered in gingham bordered with yellow rickrack. I opened it carefully. Faded pink tissue protected the contents. I folded back the tissue. There tucked carefully away was a pair of lacy underwear, obviously never worn, with a strange, handwritten note on top. It read, *Beware of ants in your pants!* I picked up the note and noticed tiny black ants. Upon closer inspection I found ants throughout the folds of underpants, carefully glued in place. *What were these doing in my mother's closet?* I wondered to myself. *Who would give my mother ants in her pants?* At fifty-three I still didn't have nerve to ask my eighty-four-year-old mother for an explanation. I started to toss the cigar box into the trash, then hesitated. What a good story, I thought, to share with my own friends. The ants and pants moved to Kansas and soon found their way to a new owner. Ontogeny continues to recapitulate phylogeny.

We sorted into piles of things to move to Kansas, things to sell at auction, things *to give to the girls,* things to throw away. It was harder on my father than my mother. Once she had made up her mind that it was time to move closer to family in Kansas, my mother was ready to pick up and go. She would put in the auction box a painting that had been on the bedroom wall for years, and then carefully pack for the trip to Kansas a plastic, glue-gunned church given to her by someone she only knew for three months. I scrambled to save our early lives as she got rid of family photos, saving only one of each child and grandchild, but she packed for Kansas stacks and stacks of towels she got for a bargain at the towel factory she visited in Georgia some thirty years earlier.

My father, on the other hand, mourned the loss of every discarded item. He studied every photo, every old letter. (He slipped to me a clipping from a high school newspaper. It looked like nothing of importance, a yellowed old ad for some remedy, but in the margins, scrawled in pencil was a note passed in class and written by his teenaged sweetheart, the girl who would become my mother. The note chastised him for smiling at someone named Nadine and warned him that he would no longer be welcome to use her notebook and pen if he continued talking to Nadine.) He tried to browse in every book. Even frayed trousers and old shirts represented lost opportunities for painting. My mother had little empathy it seemed to me at the time. Looking back a couple years later, I realize she was looking into the future, and she saw the abyss that awaits us all. It was the ultimate act of parental love to rip out the substance of their lives at the age of eighty-six and eighty-four, to spare their daughters the painful culling at the same time as the final cutting of the parental cord.

An image comes to my mind and I cannot shake it. When I was a child, we lived on Greybull Heights, out on "the Bluff," as we used to say. We had room to roam and a huge expanse of lawn lined with gigantic cottonwood trees and lilacs that bloomed in late spring. It was a fall ritual to butcher old hens for the freezer. The whole family got involved. A long assembly row of tables would be set up on the lawn. Everyone had an assignment. My father was the executioner. Usually he would grab a chicken by the neck and quickly twirl it in the air; its neck would twist and the chicken would go flying and land on the grass near the lilac bush. Terry, the boy-next-door, and I would run and shriek, caught up in some primal game to see how close we could get to the headless chicken without it flopping on us, as we watched it flail and flop in sporadic convulsions.

My mother would retrieve the chickens. She passed them off to Bea, my unofficial grandmother, who dangled the chickens by their feet as she doused them into boiling vats of water. The air was a mixture of steam and wet chicken feathers. It was early fall. The blanched chickens would then be passed farther down the tables, away from the vats of boiling water where my sisters, Terry, and I waited at our stations, ready to receive our chicken for plucking. I liked plucking chickens. I felt useful and grown up. The feathers came out easily. Once the bird was bare, it was necessary to go back over it, examining it for pin feathers. Then it was passed back to my mother for final inspection before she took the bird to the sink for disemboweling. Standing on a step stool, I would watch her remove the intestines, so many loops of pearly blue and pink and purple, I could scarcely believe they fit inside one chicken. I watched her slit open the gizzard and remove the grit. My mind flipped to the gizzard stones my father and I hunted in the hills. My mother was an expert at disemboweling. She was swift and efficient. While we on the assembly line cleaned up, my father would stand and stare at the chickens remaining in the pen. When it was all over, we would have chicken and noodles for dinner. My mother was not sentimental. She was a pragmatist.

My father was the dreamer of the family. Mother ran a competent household. My father, whom we girls called *Daddy*, was the nurturer. Mother bought me a school desk before I was old enough to go to school and stocked it with learning materials and a chalk board so I could play school. Daddy took me with him to hike the ditch and explore the pasture as he went about his irrigating duties. Mother bought me pretty dresses. Daddy placed me on the back of the garden tractor to retrieve fishing worms as he tilled the garden. Mother let me help pick green beans in the garden. Daddy made me a tire swing. Now as we picked and discarded through the assembly line of boxes that lined the yard, it seemed once again, Mother was seeing clearly the task that was before her. My father was looking back.

I began working with him on cleaning out his studio. This was the most painful task I have ever undertaken. The studio was his private space. His soul lived there. It was so full of his treasures or soon-to-be-converted-into-treasure that one could barely edge through the space. The walls were covered with paintings, both his and others he had picked up in his wanderings. Frames of all sizes and sorts were everywhere, on the walls, in boxes on the floor, stacked on cabinets. Some were still in their wrappings, others were badly in need of repair, discovered in some secondhand shop. A tabletop had a pallet filled with splotches of oil paint kept ready and wet as though he would be returning to it soon to pick up where he left off. Brushes waited in jars. A ten-gallon hat with a pheasant feather hung from the edge of an easel. On another peg was a cap that I had given him as an adult, my delayed rebellion against my proper upbringing: *If you ain't from Wyoming, you ain't shit.* Another cap near the door proclaimed, *Besome--yo soy mexicano, or "Kiss me—I'm Mexican."* One shelf had an eight-track tape player and a case of eight-track tapes.

One shelf way in the back, scarcely visible beyond the easels, had five or six collectable, ceramic water pipes my father had bought in Hawaii not realizing, my mother insisted, what their use was intended for. As far as I know, he never used them; he just liked having them. One was a big biker with long hair riding a hog, another was a clay bird, graceful and eye-catching, another was brass. My father always enjoyed breaking the rules—not the big major rules—he was a devoted Catholic and as noted earlier, a fourth degree Knight of Columbus—but he did enjoy stretching the boundaries. My father liked room to stretch.

As a child I remember visiting the Taos Pueblo. We were stopped at the entrance where visitors were expected to pay a fee for the right to "view the natives' lives." As my father rolled down the window to pay, a man leaned in and said, "You Indian?"

My father replied, "Well, sorta."

The man said, "You go on in."

He did not care what tribe we were from. We were Indian. We little girls in the backseat of the family station wagon were gleeful.

Even as adults when we would go visit the Whitney Gallery of Western Art and Buffalo Bill Museum in Cody, Wyoming, if my mother was with us, we always paid the entry fee. Sometimes, however, she would stay home and our father would take us there. Whenever we went with him, we would often be nodded through, feeling recognized as special somehow. Now when I go to Santa Fe, and if I am wandering alone without my Caucasian husband, I am sometimes surprised to find that I still get my father's special treatment. I am given my free pass.

Although we were raised to know we were of Mexican-Irish-English heritage, perhaps the strongest ties were to our Native roots. The Purépecha from my grandmother's side has always seemed the stronger pull for us. As a child I remember our visits to Mexico and our seeking out the Purépecha Indian influence as we explored Michoacán. The beautiful butterfly nets of the fishermen at Lake Pátzcuaro are magical boats etched on my mind.

Years later I was wandering through a fiesta in San Antonio when I spotted dancers in dazzling silver and turquoise regalia. I worked my way to the front of the crowd and stood mesmerized by the dancer dressed in turquoise and silver plumage. The music and dancing finally came to an end, and people dispersed into the afternoon. I was still standing there when the turquoise bird approached me. He said something to me in a language that did not sound like Spanish. It was something more ancient. A woman came up to me and said, "He is the chief and he wants to know where you are from."

"Kansas," I replied, somehow momentarily confusing Texas with Oz.

"No, no," the woman corrected. "Where are you *from*?"

By then I understood the question.

"I am Purépecha," I said, my chin up, my eyes locking on the chief's. He became animated and spoke for some moments before the woman turned to translate.

"He says to tell you," she proceeded, "that he knows you are Purépecha. He sees the *quetzal* feathers in your ears. You have the *pájaros de plata y turquesa* hanging from your ears." My hand automatically touched my earring.

"He says to tell you that the Purépecha could not be conquered. When the conquistadores came, they took all in their paths and many villages and people were destroyed, but not the Purépecha. The Purépecha survived. The Purépecha were never conquered."

I didn't have the heart to point out to him that my name was *Cortez*. But while I wear the surname of that most notorious of conquerors, I believe El Pájaro was correct. I keep this knowledge inside of me. My father carefully and quietly planted it there. I may look Kansan these days, but I know what is inside. I carry this knowledge hidden deeply inside, a secret weapon to be used against any who would break me. I am indigenous. I am ancient. I am peaceful, but I will not be conquered.

My father takes his heritage to heart. He is a quiet, unassuming man. He does not waste words. He knows what is sacred. That is why, in his studio as he and I work like busy beetles, I take his lead. We work mostly in silence. I do not discard anything without his permission. Not a rock, not a newspaper clipping. Everything is sacred, has meaning. I find the intact skeleton of a lizard in a drawer. I open a bag. Inside are eagle feathers. Eagle feathers are illegal unless you are Indian and have authority. My father found this eagle dead in his wanderings. He stopped and harvested the feathers and brought them back to his studio. He cannot throw them away, so we hide them in a box marked "KANSAS" before my mother can notice. My father and I go about our business, each in our own slight smile.

We work that way all week. My mother, growing suspicious as the week wears on, pokes her head in now and then. Her eyes never lose sight of what is in front of her. Every time she enters the studio, a few more boxes of art books get designated LIBRARY, a few more framing mats become *excessive*, a box of smooth stones collected from the creek beds, just the right size for painting, are declared *rocks*. My father's silent pain speaks to me. As soon as my mother heads back to another part of the house, we beetles get busy. I haul the rocks out to my Subaru. This creek bed is moving to Kansas. So are bags full of mats and as many art books as I can carry. We struggle to leave the grudges behind us.

Mother struggled too. A thrifty woman from the depression era, she never worried about such trivia as matching dishes on the dinner table. Not even for holidays. As a teenager it annoyed me that any nice dishes I bought her got stashed quickly away in the bottom of her china cabinet never to be seen again. We ate off melmac. I was unprepared then when Mother sat my sister, in for the weekend, and me down one day in front of the china cabinet. She had me bring out every dish and arrange according to her instruction. Then my sister and I had to pick, first one, then the other, through items of obvious value to my mother. There was Depression glass, bowls from occupied Japan and Germany. There were teapots that came with my great-grandmother when she came over from England, a fox-head relish plate with matching sugar and creamer that had belonged to my other grandmother. Aunt Nellie's pitcher. To me, they were odds and ends for the most part. For my mother, they were the history of her girlhood. The chipped pitcher she insisted go to me was not a chipped pitcher to her. It was that bright July morning her father took just her to town in the buggy and they stopped at the fair before coming home. It was the carnival game her father paid a dime to play. It was her pride when he knocked down the milk bottles and everyone clapped and slapped him on the back, and he asked her to pick whatever prize she wanted, and she didn't pick a doll like a little girl, she picked that pitcher with the navy blue Indian and navy blue tipis all around it. She picked something useful. She picked like a woman. My mother could feel the heat of the day bearing down upon her as she handed me the ceramic pitcher, its chipped spout verifying past hard times.

My father was the dreamer. He wondered. He was curious about everything. His mind was always seeking. He never met a stranger. He was genuinely interested in people. He was an artist. He sought out answers. This surely must have accounted for one of the biggest rows he and my mother ever had. It happened before they ever made the decision to uproot. I sometimes wonder in fact if it wasn't the reason Mother finally pushed for the move. She worried about our finding it after their deaths. *Without explanation.* How might it look? What would we think? What would the town think? *How could he do this to her?*

It happened this way, so my mother tells. My father was out in the garage puttering as he so often did. He always had some piece of junked equipment scrounged from who knows where that he was working over: several bicycles, an old lawnmower, a canoe. The rule was as long as he kept it out in the garage and it never came near the house, my mother wouldn't question it. He could drag home any old treasure he came across. The rule worked fine for years. Once in a while when a grandchild came to visit, an old bowling ball might find its way to the back patio but that's as close as anything got to my mother's turf. Until this day, that is, long after the actual acquisition of the thing. And it wasn't even that far from the garage. It was just out there on the lawn next to the garage while my father rearranged a little. He had every intention of putting it right back up there where it came from. Didn't my mother like to see my father cleaning, after all?

What must she have thought when, on her way out to check the garden, corn tassels and grasshoppers on her mind, she just happened to glance toward the garage, and there on the grass, right next to the garage, just east and in plain view of the neighbors' clothesline lay what could not possibly lie there in the grass: a coffin?

It certainly looked like a coffin. It was long and wooden, broader at the top and narrower at the bottom, a good six feet long. There was no other way of looking at it. It was a coffin.

"FRANK!" my mother shouted in her most commanding whisper. *"Where are you?"*

My father, closeted in the garage and lost in his machinations, heard her and immediately remembered what he had absent-mindedly left on the lawn. He knew there was no way to shine a rosy light on this. He had to step out and face the consequences. He stepped out of the shadows of the garage and into the glaring light of high noon, my mother, hands on hips, there to greet him.

"Frank," she whispered in an implied shout, "what *is* this, and what is it doing *here?*"

"Ooh," he hedged, guilt exuding like perspiration from his pores, "it's nothing. It's just something I've had up in the attic, and I just put it here while I'm rearranging. I'm going to put it back in just a minute or two."

"What are you doing with a *casket?*" There. She had finally said the word. *Casket.* Her husband of many, many years, father to her three children, grandfather of five, was hiding a casket, unbeknownst to her, in the attic of the garage. *Why would he have a casket, and how long had he had it?* Then a more pressing question occurred to her.

"Frank," she said, her voice now perfectly calm but in a low, husky tone that frightened him just a little, "is there anything *in* that casket?"

She saw the lines around his eyes tighten ever so slightly. Who was this man she had eloped to marry? Suddenly all the stories he had told over the years about Pretty Boy Floyd and the Dalton Brothers were more than legends. Maybe he did more than peek in the back window when they stopped for gas. Maybe he saw more than the sawed-off shotguns in the backseat.

No. The coffin was not that ancient, and he was just a boy back then. And she knew he couldn't have brought it with him from Kansas when he left for Wyoming to work in the fields. Everything they owned fit in one little bag and they had ten dollars between them. And they had moved between several houses since coming to Wyoming. She would have seen the coffin if he had had it then. For a minute, she almost relaxed. Then quickly the larger reality set in. *He had acquired this coffin since they had moved into this house.* What *was* he?

"Frank," she repeated, her voice getting huskier, "what is in that casket?"

My father, she had always thought, was an exceptionally moral man. He was an altar boy. He was the leader of the basketball team. He was the one who volunteered to help old ladies with their groceries. My father was a volunteer. He was civic-minded. He was a Boy Scout and later a Boy Scout leader. He liked organized activities.

My father had ever so casually managed to side-step to his right, positioning himself between the coffin and my mother.

"Now don't get upset," he started.

"Open that lid," Mother demanded. "Open it."

She felt nauseous as she planted her feet squarely in the plot of damp grass, readying herself for whatever was to happen. Hadn't she watched plenty of television? Didn't she know husbands plotted their wives' deaths all the time? Wasn't it always the quiet, neighborhood "nice guy"? Had he been in there, uninterrupted day after day, building a coffin and quietly planning her demise? He did have a hammer in his hand. Should she scream for the neighbor?

My father slowly bent over the coffin and lifted the lid. There in the bright light of day lay human remains. A skeleton. Bones yellowed with time. That skull's eye sockets looked straight through my mother, a toothy grin on his complicit face.

"Close the lid!" my mother whispered. "Close it and let's get it quickly into the garage."

As the story unfolded, my mother recalled the earlier days when they had both been involved in the Knights of Pythias, an organization built upon the principles of friendship, charity, and benevolence. My father had especially been drawn to the organization because its motto was to promote friendship among men who came together to relieve suffering. In such a small community, however, it became harder and harder to keep the organization active. Principles, it seems, are easier in theory than in practice. Eventually the organization folded. The women sorted and cataloged all of the organization's belongings. The men organized the auction to pay off the rent and utilities. Everything was sold—tables, chairs, dishes, podium, potted plants. Everything, that is, but the skeleton and coffin which was an integral part of their ceremonial activities. Was the skeleton symbolic of Damon or Pythias, each willing to lay down his life for the other? Perhaps that was not the pressing question. At the time of acquisition, long before my father joined the organization, the skeleton had been ordered through ethical channels. Now, many decades later, there were restrictions and accountability for possession of a human skeleton. Some men thought it best to dump it late at night in the city dump and cover it with refuse. Others thought that disrespectful but still thought it best to bury him in the cover of darkness. The men of good will could not agree. My father had offered to take it home with him and store it until the men could figure out how to dispose of the skeleton in a respectful and legal manner.

The men were quick to agree. Frank was a treasure. They helped him load the coffin into his covered truck, followed him back to the house, even said their hellos to my mother before heading to the garage to help my father hoist this good man into the attic, where he could rest a little closer to heaven until they figured out how to put him finally to rest. And there he stayed. And stayed.

The men quickly and conveniently forgot about the dilemma, and over time, my father sort of forgot about him too. Until this day, the day of my mother's discovery. My father had been poking around looking for some long-lost find when he happened to bump his leg into the corner of the coffin which had been long covered with a tarpaulin. He felt a pang go through him and knew he had to bring the skeleton out of the attic and deal with it. That is what he was doing when my mother ventured to check on the corn.

The skeleton issue was resolved. My father called someone in authority and the skeleton was cleared of foul play. He was free to move on. My sister was a science teacher and knew a teacher who would be thrilled to inherit the skeleton, minus the coffin. The coffin was chopped up and sent to the landfill.

This, one would think, would be the end of it, but my mother couldn't rest easy. She knew my father had been collecting and retrieving for years. She had no idea what her daughters might find one day after they were gone and no longer around to explain themselves. From that day forth, she was bent on cleaning up their history and moving to Kansas.

The dawn of the great auction the roads leading into town were lit up. Headlights announced the hoards headed toward 431 Sixth Avenue North. They came not only from Big Horn but from Washakie and Park Counties as well. Some even came in from Sheridan on the eastern side of the mountain and some came down from Billings. A small entourage came all the way from the Black Hills of South Dakota.

I am glad I could not attend. I had seen the pain my parents bravely confronted each and every day. The births of their children had happened there. They had moved from migrants to valued members of the community. My mother had educated half the town. My father had painted them. They had seen most of their friends by now to the cemetery. Sixty-four years were being auctioned off that day. Two years later, they still pour over the receipts, remarking or lamenting over how much an item brought, their only remaining way of owning it all, of making it real.

Mary Copp bought the folding rocking chair for forty dollars more than they paid for it new. She bought Oscar too. He was a bargain, one of the best portraits in my father's collections. And the Saldana girl got her grandfather Felix, the sheepherder, an old friend of my father. The riding lawn mower could have been bought for far less at the store and that old magazine rack with all its nicks and stuck in the back corner of the bedroom sold as antique for over a hundred dollars.

"It's probably foregrounded by the fireplace in somebody's McMansion," my father chuckles. "It probably holds the *Wall Street Journal* now."

The locals were having some fun with the out-of-towners. They would all bid with the dealers, pushing the prices higher and higher, then bail out at the last minute, leaving the dealer holding his paddle and owning a leaky canoe. They were laughing about that a year later.

Bill Robinson, the new game warden across the street, bought my father's Remington 30.06 bolt action for Elliott, his six-year-old, to grow into. Elliott loved my father and used to come over to play trains with him. Elliott called him "Fwank." When Bill presented the gun to Elliott, that little boy grew several inches taller, squared his shoulders as if he understood the gravity of his stewardship and reverently carried the gun home, carefully coached by his father.

It is my hope that Elliott too will learn to love the game of the Bighorns, will learn to love the land and become its guardian as he grows into my father's possession. It is my hope that all that is sacred remains.

CODA: THE WIDENING GYRE

Four years have passed since my parents moved back to Kansas. It was an adjustment. They had to make new friends as they grieved the loss of a lifetime in Wyoming. They were excited to see old acquaintances from childhood, however. They came up with a plan. They took picnic lunches to the old cemetery in hopes of running into relatives of old friends. When that didn't produce results, they started reading the obituaries regularly, and when they saw a name that was familiar, they would attend the funeral in hopes of running into people they had known as kids. They were disappointed, however, when this strategy also did not work well. Either their childhood friend was the reason for the event or they had not recognized each other, all now in their late eighties or early nineties.

Over time my parents were adjusting. They had come back home, but home was not as they had left it sixty-five years earlier. Then one cold January day, about ten thirty in the morning, I was in a meeting. An office assistant poked her head in the door and said my mother was trying to reach me. I knew this was bad news. My mother had stopped wasting her money on long distance phone calls the day my first husband graduated from college, and she had never called me at work.

As I rushed to return the call, I found myself saying, *please don't let it be bad news*, knowing as I did that it had to be bad news. My eighty-nine-year-old father had fallen. Much of the state was blanketed with ice. My parents were feeling claustrophobic and decided, against all good judgment considering that the grocery store delivered, to drive to the store. My father had gone to get the car out and had slipped on the ice in front of the garage. He was unable to get up. Fortunately for him, my mother had been watching from the window and called for help immediately.

The ambulance crew had difficulty lifting my father onto the gurney and into the ambulance because my eighty-seven-year-old mother was bent over my father kissing him repeatedly. She clung to him for life as they said their final goodbyes. My father was taken by ambulance to a larger hospital in neighboring Chanute. I was told to come immediately.

I headed out into a gloomy gray day. The further south I drove, the more desolate the drive became. Ice was everywhere. Fields were glassed over. The roads were too. Never a church-goer, I found myself once again praying, asking some Great Unknown to spare my father. I denied. I begged. I bargained. I got angry with my father for being out there in the first place. I recognized the stages of grief I had studied in school and tried to "undo" my thoughts. (Was that denial or bargaining?) I also recognized that both parents assumed he would die. My aunt had broken a hip and had surgery only to die of pneumonia during recovery.

I began to be rational, to plan ahead. Wasn't that one of the stages—acceptance? I knew whatever might happen, I had to be the adult now. I could not ride on my father's shoulders for this journey. As youngest daughter, I had always been referred to as the Baby, daughter of privilege, the spoiled one, but here I was in the Heartland, alone on this forlorn, icy journey in January.

I began to sift through my mind hunting for the tools I would need. The first order of the hunt, I remembered, was to be still. Be still and quiet. Observe what is happening around you. Read the signs. Stay calm. Interpret what you see. And above all, don't panic. Panic is a luxury only the safe can afford. I noticed, along the roadside, yellow-breasted meadowlarks picking over the pavement, looking for anything edible. They sang that intricate song that my father would sometimes imitate as we bounced along on our journeys through the badlands.

At the hospital the bad news was confirmed. A broken hip. Surgery was necessary on my eighty-nine-year-old, diabetic father. We waited most of the day by his bedside as they prepped him for surgery and monitored him for shock. He lay there, eyes closed, snoring off and on. My mother and I occupied our time with crossword puzzles, talking in muffled tones so as not to disturb my father. Late in the afternoon the orderlies and nurses prepared to move my father to surgery.

"What is a five-letter word for pony?" my mother said quietly.

"Horse," I replied, preoccupied.

"It ends with a "d," my mother said.

"A five-letter word for pony that ends with a 'd'?" I parroted. We continued to nurse this word as though it mattered.

As the orderlies rolled my father from the room, he suddenly yelled, "Pferd!"

My mother and I looked at each other, shocked. Then we all began to laugh. It was a sign. I held my father's hand briefly, transported back to the Medicine Wheel of my childhood. My father was still in control of the journey. *Pferd* was the German word for "horse."

While my father was in surgery, my mother and I sat in silence in the waiting area. I felt near panic, but when I looked at my mother, so small and diminished from the strong woman I had known all my life, I was reminded that I was the bulwark now.

I began to reflect on the words of my old friend and mentor, Dr. Norma Bunton. While she lay dying of cancer, I stayed by her bedside, sometimes the whole night long, holding her hand in silence. When the pain became too much for her and the morphine drip powerless, I would tighten my grasp on her hand and pull hard against the pain gripping her, a tug-o-war with Death itself. One particularly bad night as I stood by her bedside, I could see that there was to be no relief. Morphine was not working. She could not swallow. She seemed far off, totally unaware of my presence. Then a strong current of pain coursed through her. I fought hard to hold on to her, pulling against whatever was claiming her. She opened her eyes and saw my fear staring back at her. She hadn't spoken in days, but somehow the consummate teacher and mentor that was Norma Bunton returned.

"Don't be frightened, honey face," she said quite clearly. "This is a very valuable lesson I am teaching you." These were the last words I ever heard from her.

My father came through surgery amazingly well for his age. A few days later he was transferred to the hospital next to the retirement complex where they lived. Mother could spend her days with him. But his recovery would be slow and arduous. At eighty-nine other pesky emergencies start to accumulate. Late one night I found myself riding in an ambulance with him to the larger facility. I was five years old again, out in the middle of the badlands in the dead of night only this time he couldn't carry me on his shoulders.

"Daddy," I wanted to say, "pick me up." But he could not.

At the hospital the nurses prepped him for yet another surgery. I stayed by his side, scared, trying to be the adult, trying to be *him*. My father lay there, fully aware of his surroundings. A doctor came in and asked me to sign a form indicating whether I wanted him to be resuscitated or not.

"*Resuscitated!*" I wanted to scream, "How can you ask *me* that? Why not ask *him* that? Is he *game—just another one of my kills?*"

Quietly but firmly I heard a small girl say, "You have to ask my father to sign."

He did not have to be revived. By morning the sun was out and my father had survived. But he could not remain indefinitely at the hospital. After a few days, he was transferred to the nursing facility two blocks away from my mother.

It was here that I began to bargain again. This was the only complete-care facility in town. It was old. It was noisy, bells ringing, buzzers buzzing, an intercom's incessant pleading for help. Sheer anarchy. Shells of people sagged in wheelchairs in the hallway. Moans could be tracked down distant wings. One woman sang to a doll. Another held an endlessly banal conversation with an absent family member. The old war veteran with no family left wandered the halls saying, "Que sera, sera."

My father broke my heart every time I went there. He asked to go home. I had to refuse him. But soon, he was so medicated, he couldn't ask any more. My lovely, loving father didn't know I was there. He spent the winter there, an innocent prisoner. My mother caught pneumonia and joined him there. Things seemed to be falling apart.

By late spring they had both managed to get home again. My hundred-pound mother lifted my father in and out of bed or his recliner. I watched, helpless, as my aged parents fed their insatiable hunger, this widening desire to remain independent, their *hambres atrasadas*.

That April they celebrated their sixty-ninth wedding anniversary at the independent living apartments where they resided. All their friends and neighbors came, circling around them. My father sat in his wheelchair holding my mother's hand, newlyweds once again. The room filled with flowers, cards, balloons, and well-wishes. There was a portrait of the young couple. Women cut cake and poured punch. Cameras flashed. Everyone was hunting for the perfect memory. One man sang "Frankie and Gracie Were Lovers," then finally, "Let Me Call You Sweetheart." There they sat, turning toward one another, feeble and frail, hunting nothing, there in the center of things.

AUTHOR'S NOTE

Events depicted in this work of creative nonfiction are a combination of memory and imagination, and therefore, may be factually flawed. The terms "antelope" and "buffalo" have been used rather than "pronghorn" and "bison" because these were the terms used at the time of these events. Some names have been changed to protect those who may remember events differently. While resemblances to actual persons, living or dead, are more imagined *personnas* than actual people, the author has tried to capture the essence of the story being spun.

Lightning Source UK Ltd.
Milton Keynes UK
UKHW010651150622
404464UK00002B/358